Tricky
Business
Letters

Persuasive Tactics on Paper

▪

GORDON R. WAINWRIGHT

the Institute
of Management
PITMAN PUBLISHING

*The Institute of Management (IM) is at the forefront of
management development and best management practice.
The Institute embraces all levels of management from students
to chief executives. It provides a unique portfolio of services
for all managers, enabling them to develop skills
and achieve management excellence.
If you would like to hear more about the benefits of membership,
please write to Department P, Institute of Management, Cottingham
Road, Corby NN17 1TT. This series is commissioned by the
Institute of Management Foundation.*

Pitman Publishing
128 Long Acre, London WC2E 9AN

A Division of Longman Group UK Limited

First published in 1993

© Gordon R. Wainwright 1993

A CIP catalogue record for this book can be
obtained from the British Library

ISBN 0 273 60162 8 (Paperback)
ISBN 0 273 60407 4 (Cased)

Photoset in Linotron Century Schoolbook by
Northern Phototypesetting Co. Ltd., Bolton
Printed by Bell and Bain Ltd, Glasgow

Contents

∎

Index of letters

■

Introduction

■

Letters are one of the essential features of modern business. They bring us business, they bring us problems, they bring us information and they bring many of us to the verge of despair. This last is because, no matter how professional we might be in our own field of expertise, very few of us are professional writers. For us, writing letters – indeed, any kind of writing – is a chore. It is something that we have to do, but it is not something we enjoy.

It is because of this that this book offers over 150 letters for all sorts of tricky business occasions to make life easier and more productive. Using these letters, suitably adapted where necessary to meet your own specific requirements, will help you to get your own way more of the time.

This book offers more than simply a collection of ready-made letters for those situations that can leave the average business person tearing his or her hair out trying to find just the right way to put things. It offers in the first chapter a guide to effective letter writing which distils in one easily digestible step the current wisdom on the subject. It also offers help for all the other tricky letters that you need but that the book, because everyone's requirements are unique, could not foresee.

To make the book easy to use, there are two indexes. One (at the front) lists the letters by topic. The other lists key words and phrases to guide you quickly and precisely to the letter that will meet your needs.

Before you embark upon the search for the letter that is for you, however, there is one very important question you must ask: is a letter necessary? There are many occasions when a face to face meeting or a telephone call may be the better solution. Letters are necessary when face to face discussions have failed. They are necessary when it is important to have a permanent record of something. They are necessary to follow up on discussions for confirmation purposes.

Personal contact is better when exploring a subject or a problem for the first time. It is better when it will speed up the communication process. It is better when written words are not really suited to the task as in many problems with personal relationships at work. So, before you write that letter, ask yourself if that is indeed the best way to proceed.

If you decide that it is, this book should solve your difficulties in expressing yourself clearly and effectively. Far too often in writing letters, people feel that they have to impress rather than express. This book takes the view that tricky situations are not solved by being devious and evasive. If I had to express the essential message succinctly, it would be that in order to produce effective and persuasive letters you should make them simple, positive, active and concise. I hope that all the letters here possess those elements. If you follow the principles upon which they rest you will not only make your letters more effective, but also all the other memos, reports and business documents you have to write.

You will notice that, in the letters which follow, I have used both round brackets ( ) and square brackets [ ]. Round brackets indicate that what lies between them is part of the text. Square brackets mean that you will have to enter the relevant information at that point.

Techniques of effective letter writing

In any kind of writing the real secret of success lies not so much in the actual writing itself as in preparation and planning. If you do these properly, you will avoid many of the problems which might arise during the writing. Careful editing afterwards should remove any that do remain.

The first step, then, in writing is to prepare for the task. This means that, before you begin to collect together the information you will need for the letter, you should have the answers to three questions:

■ What is the subject of the letter?

■ Who will read it?

■ Why are you writing it?

Let us take the first question first. Unless you are clear in your own mind what it is that you wish to know or what it is you wish to tell your reader, there is very little chance that the reader will gain a clear impression. There will be confusion rather than clarity at the other end of the communication line. So pause and think what it is that will form the subject matter of the letter. Consider how much information it will contain; that is, how much detail you need to go into.

Secondly, be sure you know who will read the letter. The more you know about the recipient the better. It is always easier, after all, to write to someone you know well than it is to a perfect stranger. If you do not know the reader at all, see if it is possible to find out who it will be and if you can speak to them first. This will not always be possible or appropriate, but where it is it will give you an advantage.

It will be useful to know what the reader knows about the subject of the letter already and whether they have any strong opinions or

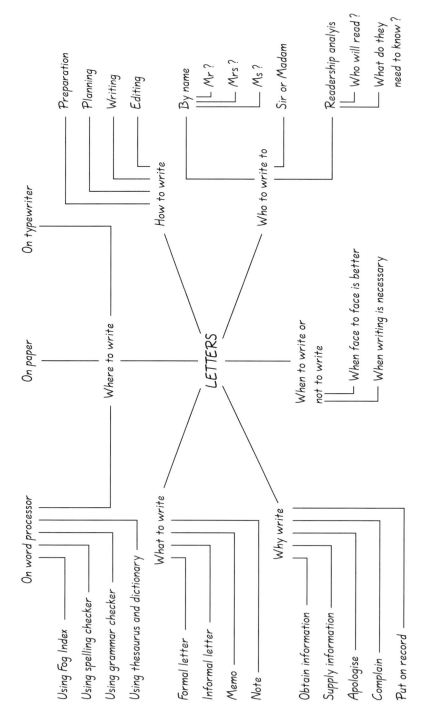

Figure 1 Example of a mind map

feelings about the topic. It is also worth considering whether anyone else will read the letter. The more you know about them as well, the better. If you are giving information, ask yourself what the reader really needs to know. There is little point in putting information into letters simply because you possess it. Everything that is in the letter should only be there because the reader needs it.

Consider the response or reaction you require from your readers. Unless you are clear about this, there is less chance that they will be clear about what they are supposed to do or think. You also need to decide whether you wish to maintain a very formal relationship with your readers or a very informal one. Normally, it will be somewhere between these extremes, but you need to be sure about it.

Thirdly, you should be very clear about your objective in writing the letter. It is worth writing down the purpose of the letter in one sentence so that you have it to refer to. Again, unless you are clear about why you are writing, it is highly unlikely that the reader will be clear. Clarity in letter writing is of particular importance because many people have a lot of letters to deal with and they cannot give each and every one a leisurely treatment. They want to be able to reply to them quickly and accurately.

3

Once you have the answers to these three questions, you can then more speedily and more effectively assemble the relevant information. In doing this essential part of preparation, you may find it useful to use two simple techniques of information gathering that many kinds of writers find useful.

They go by various names, but the first is usually referred to these days as a 'mind map'. Some people call this a spidergraph or spidergram, some a recall tree, others spray notes or scatter notes or patterned notes. It is simply an alternative method of making notes to the one that most people use. In making notes, most people make lists of points. Now lists are very fine, but they do suffer from at least two disadvantages. There is always the tendency to regard the items at the top of the list as more important than those further down. There is a hierarchical feel about a list. Also, the longer the list is, the more difficult it becomes to see inter-relationships between various points. A mind map overcomes problems like these by, instead of starting at the top of a page and working downwards, as you do with lists, beginning in the middle of the page and radiating outwards with a line for each aspect of the topic. Figure 1 gives an example of a mind map.

You will find that the mind mapping technique works particularly well if it is combined with another simple technique which again goes by various names. Some people call it 'self-recitation', some call it the journalist's questions and others refer to it as Mr Kipling's serving men. You may recall, if you did any poetry at school, that Rudyard Kipling had a little rhyme which ran:

> I keep six honest serving men,
> They taught me all I knew.
> Their names are WHAT? and WHY? and WHEN?
> And HOW? and WHERE? and WHO?'

You can probably see why they are called the journalist's questions because they cover all the angles. When you ask the question WHAT? you are automatically looking for information about events, actions or things. Ask the question WHY? and you are looking for reasons, conclusions, deductions, inferences and implications. Ask WHEN? and you are clearly interested in time factors. Ask HOW? and you are looking for information about method or methods or processes. Ask WHERE? and you seek information about place or location and ask WHO? and you are looking for information about people. You can even use each of these questions on each initial branching out from the centre of the mind map. The example of a mind map on letter writing on page 3 shows you how you might use some of these questions as a basis for your own mind maps.

Many people find it useful at this point to pause in the process of writing a letter. Do something else for a few minutes – make a telephone call, see someone about something else or have a coffee – and then return and look through what you have done up to this point. This short break, or incubation period, enables you to look at your handiwork with a degree of objectivity. The problem in checking your own work is that you always tend to see what you intended to put rather than what is actually there. Incubation periods help you to overcome this problem.

Once you have collected your information together, you can turn to the task of structuring it. Every letter needs a structure. It is no use sitting down and starting writing, putting things down in the order in which they come into your head. If you have used mind mapping and self-recitation, you will find that this has begun the process of structuring for you quite automatically by grouping similar items together.

Decide the form of the letter at this point. Will it be formal or informal? Will it require a heading, as most business letters do? Will you address the reader by name or simply as Dear Sir or Dear Madam? Will you use all the information you have to hand or will you need to be selective on the basis of relevance and the reader's need to know? Will there be any additional material or enclosures to accompany the letter?

We can go further. Decide how many paragraphs the letter will have. You will need one for the opening and one for the closing, of course. But what of the body of the letter? Remember that paragraphs are not random collections of sentences. Every paragraph should deal with a separate aspect of the subject. So you need to consider how many sections your information breaks down into and have a paragraph for each one.

5

Even though you will not use them in a letter, it is helpful to give each section a heading. In most letters, there will only be two or three. Nevertheless, they will help you to see the logical basis on which you have organised your information and the logical progression within the structure. Many people simply plan the letter in their heads, but I think it is always useful, and especially so with tricky letters, to have the headings to refer to in case unexpected difficulties arise during the writing.

Once you have a good, detailed plan, you should find that the letter virtually writes itself. Time spent planning is not additional time, it is time, as it were, transferred from the writing stage into the planning stage. Overall, the process of writing a letter should become noticeably quicker as well as more effective.

Decide how you will begin the letter. Will you address your reader as Mr, Mrs or Ms? It is best to find out in advance, if you can, which they prefer. Some people have strong feelings on this point whilst others do not. There are, however, no strict rules on which it should be. Nor are there rules on when to move from a formal tone with a reader to a less formal tone. I think the best guide is to let your correspondent make the first move in making matters more informal between you, especially if you are more concerned to please them than they might be to please you. There is a list of the most common ways of addressing various kinds of people in the Forms of Address section on page 183.

When it comes to actually writing the letter, write a first draft. Do not try to make the letter perfect as you go. Many people do. They try to get the letter just right sentence by sentence and paragraph by paragraph as they proceed. This approach suffers from two disadvantages. It is slow and it is not very effective. It is not very effective because as you write you are always dealing with an incomplete context until you get right to the end of the letter. This means that it is easy enough to see the effect of a change on what is already written down, but it is very difficult, if not impossible, to see the effect on what is yet to come. Write a first draft which you will then edit and these are no longer problems.

Write the letter at a single sitting wherever possible. The reason for this is that there is then a much greater chance that you will finish with the same concept in mind of what it is you are trying to achieve as you had when you started. The longer the period over which things are written, the more likely it is that you will perhaps slightly, but significantly, change your mind. This confusion on your part is bound to transmit itself to the reader. You do not want that to happen.

As you write, follow the principles and techniques of effective writing that apply whatever it is you are producing, be it a letter, memo, report or other document. The first principle is to have a systematic approach. If you follow the advice given in this chapter, you will have that because you will prepare before you plan, you will plan before you write and you will write before you edit. When you think about it, this is a natural process and it is surprising that more people do not follow it. After all, you have to collect your information before you can organise it. You cannot organise what you do not have. You really should organise what you write before you write it rather than simply diving straight in. You cannot edit before you have written.

Within this systematic approach, the key stage is the one we discussed above: planning. Proper planning prevents poor performance, as they say. It establishes your pattern of organisation and enables you then to decide more easily upon matters like paragraphing and sentence construction. Generally speaking, paragraphs should be short, but not too short. As a reasonable rule of thumb, they should be between about three sentences and six in length. If they are shorter than three sentences, they may be single sentence paragraphs and these should be saved for points you particularly wish to emphasise. If they are longer than six sentences, they may put the reader off. Most readers do not like long words, long sentences or long paragraphs. Do you?

Within sentences, you need to consider carefully the words you will use. The collections of letters which comprise the bulk of this book should be a considerable help to you in this.

Once you have paid proper attention to these major principles of effective writing, it becomes much easier to solve any problems you may have with the techniques of putting your points over. For instance, if you are writing short sentences, say less than 20 words on average, you are less likely to experience grammatical problems. You need long sentences to make things grammatically complex. Short sentences benefit from the simple fact that the less there is to go wrong, the less likely things are to go wrong.

7

If you are writing short sentences, you need less punctuation so you will have fewer punctuation problems. There will be no need to agonise over whether you should use a colon or a semicolon. You will solve the problem by avoiding it. Moreover, if you choose short words as well wherever you can, you will have fewer spelling problems. Of all the people I know who cannot spell 'accommodation' (they use one 'm' instead of two), I do not know anyone who cannot spell 'hotel', 'house', 'flat', 'room' or whatever the context requires.

There are other, more practical considerations you should bear in mind. You should try to avoid tautologies. This is simply the technical term for unnecessary repetitions of words, as in a sentence like, 'You should avoid the repetition and restatement of points in letters.' Clearly, you do not need both 'repetition' and 'restatement' here; one of them will suffice.

You should always try to use the active voice rather than the passive voice. Once grasped, the distinction should be easy to remember. In the active voice, for instance, something does something to, for, about, etc. something else. In the passive voice, something is done to, for, about, etc. something. An example of the active voice is, 'You should take extra care when editing your writing.' An example of the passive voice is, 'Extra care should be taken when editing your writing.'

Recent research has shown that the brain has to work harder when reading passive statements than when reading active statements. If you impose extra work upon your readers, they become less likely to respond as you want them to. You should always remember that you are writing for your readers; they are not reading for you.

None of this is to argue, of course, that you should never use the passive voice. There are occasions when, perhaps to achieve a more formal tone, it becomes necessary. We must remember, however, that using the passive voice will cost us some potential loss of clarity, especially if the reader is not a particularly efficient one.

For similar reasons, you should try to avoid qualifying phrases or statements wherever you can. In that sentence, 'wherever you can' is an example of a qualifying statement. Give the reader as clear a run at the subject as possible. Take care to ensure that you know the meanings of the words you use. I once received a letter which contained the statement, 'We shall need to interface on this point.' The writer meant 'meet', but had taken a fashionable term from computer language and misused it.

Remember that each sentence should have one subject and each paragraph should deal with a single topic or aspect of a topic. If you try to cram more than you should into a sentence, you may find you have written something like, 'We did have six delegates carried forward to July, two have requested to go through to October, two have now left the companies they were with and no longer require the course, and we can't obviously run a course with the remaining two.' I received that in a letter from an organisation specialising in training secretaries in, among other things, letter writing. You might have a moment's diversion deciding what else is wrong with the sentence apart from trying to deal with too many points at once.

Above all, keep the reader in mind all the time as you write. Rather than ask: 'How can I put this into words?' ask yourself: 'What is the best way for the reader to understand this?' Focus on the reader and the reader's problems and somehow this seems to draw the right words out. It is always easier, after all, to solve someone else's problems than your own.

Once you have written the letter, put it on one side for as long as you reasonably can. Sometimes, this will only be for a few minutes. On other occasions, you may be able to leave it overnight. The more important the letter, the longer this incubation period needs to be because the longer it is, the more objective you can be when you return to it.

We come now to the final stage: editing. Here, you need to look at your work as critically as you can to remove any remaining errors and to bring about further improvements where you can identify these. You may find it helpful to use the checklist below when you do this.

CHECKLIST FOR EFFECTIVE LETTERS

1 Have you kept the reader in mind and written for him or her?

2 Have you repeated anything unnecessarily?

3 Have you overlooked any details?

4 Are there any parts where what you have written is ambiguous?

5 Does the heading accurately reflect the content of the letter?

6 Does the letter read smoothly and follow a logical progression?

7 Do any statements contradict each other?

8 Is it clear which statements are facts and which are opinions?

9 Have you justified any conclusions drawn or recommendations made by supporting them with the relevant facts?

10 Have you checked the Fog Index (see below)?

11 Going through the letter in detail, can you omit anything without affecting the meaning?

12 Have you avoided jargon as far as possible?

13 If you received this letter, would you know exactly what to do about it?

14 Have you checked grammar, punctuation and spelling, using where appropriate a computer program?

15 Is the layout correct (see the example letters in the following chapters)?

16 Is the language free from slang?

17 Is all the information given accurate and verifiable?

18 Is the purpose of the letter clear?

19 Have you kept the letter as simple as possible, without over-simplifying?

20 Are you completely satisfied with the letter? Even if you are, check it again if there is time.

9

You may also find it useful to calculate the Fog Index of your text. This is a means of assessing quickly the level at which you have pitched the letter. You take the actual text of the letter only. Count how many words you have written. Count the number of sentences. Count the number of words which have more than six letters. Calculate the average sentence length (the number of words divided by the number of sentences). Calculate the percentage of long words (the number of long words divided by the number of words altogether, multiplied by 100). Add the average sentence length and the percentage of long words and multiply by 0.4 (for example, $0.4\,[20 + 10] = 12$). According to research, the figure you end up with roughly equates to the number of years of full-time education someone will need to have had in order to read what you have written with reasonable ease and efficiency. A figure of 10–12 is generally regarded as 'safe' and below 10 is 'easy'.

It is not necessary, of course, to calculate the Fog Index for everything you write, but it can be useful if the letter is a particularly important one in the sense that you wish it to make a good impression when it is read. It is also worth calculating the Fog Index on standard letters and memos. For some reason, when people draft standard letters, they use the passive voice more often and they use more long words than normal. This usually results in longer sentences which increase the Fog Index.

Before you send the letter, you may wish, if there is time, to put it on one side again and then run a further check just to be sure. In other words, at this point it is rather like being back in the school examination room. Remember the age old advice most of us will have received. You never leave early: if you finish early, check, check and check again. If you can, get someone else to check the letter with you. It is always easier for them to spot errors or parts to improve. You will always have the problem that we discussed earlier of seeing what you intended to put rather than what you actually did put.

If you produce your letters yourself on a word processor, or even if someone else does it for you, it is worth bearing in mind that these days there are various programs available which can help a writer a great deal. Most word processing packages, for instance, contain a spelling checker. Even if you are a good speller, these can help you to spot typographical errors that might otherwise slip through. Many packages also contain a thesaurus and a dictionary which can be useful if you are looking for alternative words or want to check on the meaning of a word. Some will also calculate the Fog Index and other measures of readability for you. It is worth looking around for one that does all of the things you want it to. Many computer magazines aimed at the general reader contain regular reviews of what various programs will do and how well they do them.

There are also a growing number of grammar checkers on the market and two in particular are useful. One is called 'StyleWriter' and is recommended by the Plain English Campaign. This claims to check for over 20,000 possible grammatical errors. The other is 'Grammatik', currently in its fifth version. The main difference between the two is that 'Grammatik' allows you to make on-screen corrections, whilst 'StyleWriter' gives you a print-out to check and you then make your changes using your normal word processing package. This means that 'Grammatik' tends to suit those who do their own word processing and 'StyleWriter' suits those who have their word processing done by someone else, say a secretary.

11

If you follow the systematic approach described in this chapter and you obey the more practical points when you are doing the actual writing, you should find that your letter writing becomes not only more effective but also quicker. Time, after all, is a limited commodity and anything which will help us to make better use of it will be welcome. The rest of this book now gives you ready-made letters for tricky business situations. For each one, I have added comments on why I have written the letter in the way that I have. I hope you find the letter you need. I should, however, welcome suggestions for any tricky letters I have omitted. I can then deal with these in future editions. Write to me care of the publishers.

Customers and Clients

2.1 REPLYING TO AN ANGRY CUSTOMER

Dear Mr Watson

I was very sorry to hear that you have had problems with [name and model of product].

This product usually performs reliably and has always performed exceptionally well in the quality tests which we carry out regularly on all our products. I have checked our records and we have had no difficulties similar to the ones you have experienced.

As I am unable to tell from your description of the faults you have identified whether these were caused by defects in the product or inappropriate use, I should like to suggest that you send the item to me. When our engineers have inspected it, I shall be in a better position to state what we could do to ensure that you were satisfied with its performance.

I enclose a prepaid postal bag for your use.

Yours sincerely

Comment

With this type of letter, you have to recognise that, for the customer, this is a big problem. The customer expects action. The customer is angry. People who are angry, for whatever reason, not only do not always express themselves clearly, but are more than usually likely to misinterpret what is said or written to them.

You need, therefore, to apologise immediately in such a way that you are not admitting liability. You need to reassure. You need to devise some means of establishing the true facts. In this case, the suggestion is that the customer returns the item for investigation. A prepaid postal bag is less costly than having a disgruntled customer out there sounding off to any willing ears about how bad your products are.

There could be a heading on the letter between the 'Dear . . .' and the text, but leaving the heading out tends to make the letter less formal and more personal. The closer you can get to your reader, without being too casual, the more likely they are to regard you as a friend rather than an enemy.

13

2.2 AN APOLOGY FOR ACTION NOT TAKEN WHICH SHOULD HAVE BEEN TAKEN

Dear Mr Marshall

Thank you very much for your letter of [date], concerning our failure to [briefly describe action not taken].

We try extremely hard to maintain the highest possible levels of service to our customers. In this instance, it seems we have failed. Please accept my most sincere apologies for this. I can assure you that we have already taken steps to ensure that it cannot happen again.

I hope you will realise that our lack of response on this occasion is not typical of our treatment of our customers. Please write to me personally should you have any cause to complain about our service in the future.

Yours sincerely

14

Comment

You need a brief introductory paragraph to show that you are fully aware of what it is that you have not done.

Since you are clearly in the wrong, there is little point in trying to brazen it out. There are still people around who say that you should never admit liability for anything. Modern standards of customer care, however, dictate that you should, unless there is a possibility that by doing so you would leave yourself open to legal proceedings.

You do need to apologise and to show that you have taken action to prevent a recurrence of the problem.

An appeal for clemency in the final paragraph, coupled with the offer of a direct line of contact should the need arise, should help to make the reader a little less antagonistic towards you.

Once again, the absence of a heading makes the letter a little more personal and a little less formal.

2.3 CUSTOMER DELAYING A DECISION

Dear Mr Sleightholme

Proposed purchase of [state item]

I am very pleased that you have shown interest in our [state item], which we can supply on most competitive terms. I had hoped that we might have received a firm order by now, but this does not seem to have happened.

It may be, of course, that you have changed your mind and decided to buy something else. However, if you are still interested in [state item], but would like further information, a demonstration, or a review of the purchase terms, please contact me.

I look forward to hearing from you in the very near future.

Yours sincerely

15

Comment

Here we wish to renew contact with a customer and prompt them to act, but not in such a way that they feel we are taking up their time unnecessarily. This would only irritate them. So a heading will be useful because it will tell the reader immediately why we are writing and then, if they are too busy to attend to the letter straight away, they are more likely to put it to one side for later attention than to drop it in the bin.

The first paragraph needs to be encouraging with a slight tone of reproach. The second needs to offer the reader a choice of responses. There is no point in trying to back the reader into a corner. The final one should encourage without badgering.

2.4 ENCOURAGING A SLOW PAYER TO MAKE PAYMENT

Dear Mr Robson

<u>Account no. [state reference]</u>

I have noted that this account is now considerably overdue. As you know, our terms are payment within [number] days and this account dates from [date].

If you have a problem with this account, please contact me as soon as possible, so that we may resolve the difficulty.

If you are happy with the details of the amount due, I should very much appreciate a cheque by return. If this is not possible, again, please contact me so that we may discuss the situation.

This letter may have crossed your payment in the post, in which case please disregard it and accept my thanks for settling the account.

Yours sincerely

16

Comment

This letter requires a heading because it needs to be a little more formal. It will also help the reader to identify quickly which unpaid bill you are referring to.

The first paragraph should be quite specific about how much is owed and for how long. If you have specific credit terms, it is useful to restate these here.

Rather than threaten the reader with dire consequences immediately, it can be useful to suggest a possible reason for the delay in payment. Then offer them a choice of actions – pay up or say why not. Finally, in case they may already have sent payment and it is still in the post or your own accounts department, do not apologise for sending the letter (which many people do), but tell them to disregard it and thank them for the payment.

2.5 GREETING A NEW CUSTOMER OR CLIENT

Dear Mrs Robertson

Many thanks for placing your first order with us. I hope that all the items meet with your full satisfaction. If you have any cause at all for complaint, please contact me so that we may put matters right.

Naturally, we are always pleased to welcome new customers/clients [select which is most appropriate] and we look forward to a long and happy association with you. We value your custom just as much as we do that of our long standing customers/clients [select one].

Please contact me personally at any time if there are any problems in your dealings with us.

Yours sincerely

17

Comment

This kind of letter needs to be as personal as you can make a business letter. For this reason, it is probably better not to have a heading. A lot of people regard letters with headings almost as if they were official letters. However, if the new customer is another business then a heading will do no harm and may even assist slightly with speed of filing.

Express your gratitude; after all, new customers are like gold dust these days. Give them an immediate helpline should they ever need it. The second paragraph should make it seem as if they are almost being welcomed into a very friendly club. Finally, a repetition of the confirmation of their direct access to a friend in times of trouble will reinforce your commitment to customer after-care.

2.6 TRYING TO RECOVER A LOST CUSTOMER

Dear Ms Briggs

I have looked through our customer/client [select as appropriate] lists and I note that it is some time since you placed an order with us. I hope this does not mean that we have lost your custom entirely.

I have no record of receiving any complaint from you about our products/services [select as appropriate], but if you have any cause for dissatisfaction I should very much like to know about it. We pride ourselves on maintaining the highest standards of customer service and, if we have failed to meet these standards in any way, we should very much like to have the opportunity of remedying matters.

Please contact me personally if you have any complaint about our products/services [select one] or if there is any other way in which I can be of help.

Yours sincerely

Comment

Once again, we wish to establish as close a personal contact with this lost customer as we can, so the letter has no heading.

The first paragraph should show concern without panic or strong reproof. The second should gently prod the reader to respond in some way and the last should offer the direct line again.

Lost customers are usually lost forever, but a letter showing genuine interest and concern in finding out why they have gone elsewhere may produce a response which, if it does not actually bring the customer back, may help you to identify a way of avoiding losing other customers in the future.

18

2.7 REFUSAL OF CREDIT

Dear Mr Smith

Application for a Credit Account

Thank you for your application for a credit account with this company.

Before we set up a credit account with any customer, it is our policy to undertake the usual commercial checks of credit rating and we did, of course, carry these out in your case. Unfortunately, from the sources we use we have been unable to establish a satisfactory credit rating in your case. This may be due to a number of reasons. For instance, you may not have applied for a credit account with anyone else previously.

In the circumstances, however, I am unable to set up a credit account in your name at this time. We shall always, of course, be pleased to supply goods/services [select as appropriate] on a cash with order basis.

19

If you do place such orders with us, I shall review your application for a credit account in six months' time.

Yours sincerely

Comment

This letter needs to be more formal than some of the previous ones. You are turning someone down, probably for very good reasons, so you do not want to get too close and familiar. For this reason, the opening paragraph is quite terse.

The second paragraph can then be more informative and helpful by being quite specific, without going into too much possibly embarrassing detail, about the reasons for the refusal.

By the third paragraph, the reader is braced for the bad news. You need to be polite, firm, but not dismissive and therefore you indicate that you are still prepared to do business.

The final paragraph offers a review in six months' time. The fact that this review will in many cases produce the same result does not matter. You will be seen to have acted fairly and the promise therefore costs you nothing.

2.8 APOLOGY FOR SENDING INCORRECT GOODS

Dear Mrs Hogg

Order no. [state reference]

Thank you very much for your letter of [date], concerning inaccuracies in your order.

Please accept my sincere apologies for our error, which was due to [state reason].

We have now sent the items you requested and because you have suffered inconvenience, I enclose [small gift] which I hope you will accept with our compliments.

We process large numbers of orders every day and, whilst we try to maintain the highest standards of efficiency, mistakes do sometimes occur. It is our policy that, when this rare event happens, we do our utmost to ensure that the customer is satisfied with the corrected order. Please contact me personally if you have any further cause for complaint.

Yours sincerely

Comment

The apology here needs to be made early and needs to be accompanied by an appropriate explanation of why the error occurred. Action should have been taken and it is not a bad idea to enclose something by way of a sweetener to compensate slightly for the inconvenience caused.

The final paragraph admits that things can go wrong in the most efficient of businesses. It reassures the customer that he or she is an important person to you and again offers a direct line of contact if matters are still not in order.

2.9 APOLOGY FOR DELAY IN SENDING GOODS

Dear Mr White

Order no. [state reference]

Thank you very much for your letter of [date], concerning the delay in sending the goods you ordered on [date].

I am very sorry that we have inconvenienced you in this way. We always try to send goods within the period stipulated in our advertising. However, on this occasion we failed to meet that objective. I hope you will accept the enclosed [small gift] as a token of our sincere regret that you did not receive the goods by the expected date.

The delay in sending was caused by [state reason briefly]. I recognise that this is no adequate excuse, but you should by now have received the items you ordered and I hope they meet your requirements.

If there is anything further I can do to ensure that you are entirely happy now with our service, please contact me.

Yours sincerely

21

Comment

Once more an early apology is needed, together with an admission of falling short of expected standards. A small sweetener might also help to stave off annoyance on the part of the customer.

It is important to find out why the delay occurred, so that you can ensure it does not happen to other customers if at all possible, and to tell this customer what the reasons were. Again, you need to be sure that action has been taken to get the goods to the customer as quickly as possible.

Just in case there are any further problems, give the customer a named person to contact. People do not usually like dealing with anonymous individuals these days.

2.10 APOLOGY FOR POOR SERVICE

Dear Mr Campbell

I was very sorry to learn that our service did not meet your expectations as we do pride ourselves on our reputation for caring for customers/clients [select as appropriate].

I have made enquiries and find that you were fully justified in pointing out that we had failed to [brief statement of failure]. I hope that it will not prevent you from using our services in the future.

I can assure you that I shall personally make sure that your future dealings with us will proceed smoothly and efficiently. To that end, I should be most grateful if you will send your future requirements marked for my attention. In this way, I can ensure that you receive the quality of service that you require.

Yours sincerely

Comment

Since this needs to be a personal response to the customer, you might omit a heading and also maintain an 'I – you' viewpoint to emphasise this.

If you have indeed given poor service, this is best admitted – the customer knows it anyway – and you should give a brief explanation of the reason.

Assure the customer of your personal commitment, or that of a named individual, to their future satisfaction with your standards of service and give them a contact just in case they need it.

2.11 DEALING WITH A JUSTIFIED COMPLAINT

Dear Mr Hobbs

Your complaint about [give brief details] has been passed to me for attention. I am very sorry that you have been inconvenienced by our failure to provide the level of service to which you are entitled.

I have made enquiries and found that the problem was caused by [give brief details]. I can assure you that we have taken steps to make sure that this kind of situation cannot arise again.

Please accept the enclosed [small gift] as a token of our apology and appreciation of your highly valued custom. Please contact me personally if you experience any problems with our services in the future.

Yours sincerely

23

Comment

This is another letter which requires a more personal approach and therefore does not really need a heading.

You should give an apology early in the letter and then show that you have indeed taken the complaint seriously. A small gift, which could be one of your promotional materials such as a pen, calendar or small piece of office equipment, will help to take the sting out of the complaint and show that you are sincere in your apology. It is the common practice of British Rail, for instance, when replying to customers' complaints about poor service, to include travel vouchers worth between £5 and £20 if they feel complaints are justified.

2.12 DEALING WITH AN UNJUSTIFIED COMPLAINT

Dear Ms Pearson

[Subject of complaint]

Thank you for your letter of [date], concerning [brief details of complaint].

I have thoroughly investigated this complaint and have interviewed all the staff involved. I can, however, find no evidence to support the claims that you made. Indeed, I am satisfied that our staff acted properly and with due courtesy and efficiency.

I hope that you will accept my regret that you feel we were remiss in our dealings with you. If, however, you can give me any evidence to support your claims, I shall be pleased to review the situation. If you would like to discuss the matter in person, please contact me directly.

Yours sincerely

Comment

Here we do not need to be quite so personal and therefore we might well have a heading.

The tone needs to be polite but firm and, even though the complaint is not justified, you will still need to show that you have taken it seriously. An expression of regret is appropriate and you should give the complainant the opportunity to furnish any further evidence he or she might not have already given you.

The offer of a face to face discussion of the matter will in all probability not be taken up, since once people have got a complaint off their chest they often lose interest in it, but it is still worth making. If it is taken up, it will help you to establish more firmly whether or not there is any real substance to be dealt with.

2.13 AFTER-SALES LETTER

Dear Mr Gardner

It is now a month since you purchased [item] from us and I thought I would write to ask if you were completely satisfied with the product. It is, of course, fully guaranteed should anything go wrong, but we do like to know that customers are happy with their purchases.

As you know, we do offer a full range of [items] and should you require more information about any of them, please contact me personally.

I look forward to hearing from you if we can be of any assistance.

Yours sincerely

Comment

A personal approach without a heading and an 'I – you' viewpoint is appropriate here. It is important not to be too pushing in tone. You are simply checking that everything is all right. At least, that is what the customer should think. In reality, you are seeking to lay the basis for the next sale.

Give the customer a direct line to yourself or a named individual and, finally, encourage them to come forward, but do not press the point too firmly.

25

2.14 CLIENT IN BREACH OF CONTRACT

Dear Mr Jones

Breach of contract

As you know, our contract with you required that you [give brief details].

I have been informed by [name] that you are not complying with the following clause/s:

[Give details]

I should be grateful therefore if you would arrange to comply fully with all the terms of the contract by [date].

If you have any problems in fulfilling this requirement, please contact me personally immediately so that we can discuss the matter.

Yours sincerely

Comment

This is clearly a serious matter and one which needs to be handled carefully. In this kind of letter you should be careful not to threaten any kind of action which you do not fully intend to carry out.

It is important to be as specific as possible and to set a reasonable deadline by when the client should respond. People who do not stick to the terms of contracts tend also to be tardy in responding to efforts to make them conform.

Your tone should be fairly formal and quite firm, without being aggressive. There should be a clear implication that you mean business and the client should be able to work out for himself or herself what the likely steps are that you will take if he or she does not adhere to the contract in future. At this stage, unless you are dealing with someone who has a history of not keeping to contracts, you do not need to threaten legal action, for example.

2.15 TO A CLIENT WHO HAS CLOSED AN ACCOUNT

Dear Mrs Wilkinson

Account no. [give details]

Thank you for your letter of [date] closing your account with us.

I was very sorry to learn that you were unhappy with the service you have received from us. I can assure you that the experiences you had are not typical of the service we try to provide for our customers.

I would hope that, even at this late stage, you might reconsider your decision and give us another chance to prove that our standards of service are of the highest in the industry.

If you would like to discuss this possibility further, please contact me personally. I can assure you that I shall do everything in my power to ensure that you are satisfied with our service.

27

Yours sincerely

Comment

This is a delicate situation because the last thing you want to do is invite a whole volume of complaint and recrimination upon your head. It is worth the risk, though, if you are pretty sure that this person's experience is not typical of that undergone by most of your customers or clients.

2.16 APOLOGISING FOR AN ACCOUNTING ERROR

Dear Ms Kendall

You deserve an explanation for what went wrong in our accounting department and I hope that this letter will help resolve our recent difficulties.

I know that you can appreciate the fact that it has taken some time to find out exactly what occurred and, therefore, please accept our apologies for the delay in this response.

Apparently, your payment was received on time, but it was credited to an account which bears a similar name to yours. Therefore, we began sending you our standard notices requesting payment, in keeping with our routine policy. Even after the posting error was rectified, our accounting department failed to notify our credit department, which is why you continued to receive our correspondence demanding payment.

I know how exasperating this has been for you and I am deeply sorry that it has taken so long to straighten out this problem. While there is a procedure within our firm to preclude this type of error from occurring, we are reinforcing this procedure.

You have been a valued customer of ours for a long time and we appreciate the business we have received from you.

Yours sincerely

Comment

What makes this situation tricky is the obvious breakdown in communication between departments. You may feel that you do not need to expose this weakness to the customer, but you have to provide some kind of acceptable explanation for what has gone wrong. Everybody knows that communication failure can occur even in the best run organisation. You are far better to be completely open and honest with your complainant than to fabricate some artificial story which, in all probability, they will not believe anyway.

2.17 WELCOMING A NEW BUSINESS TO THE AREA

Dear Mr Maddison

Please accept our congratulations and best wishes for your success in your new enterprise.

Our purpose in writing this letter is to welcome you to the community and familiarise you with our service.

We provide [service] to many small businesses in the area and will be happy to arrange to have one of our sales representatives call on you.

As our way of welcoming you, we have enclosed a certificate which entitles you to a [10 per cent (10%)] discount on your first order placed with our firm.

We will look forward to seeing you.

Yours sincerely

Comment

It may seem to be a straightforward enough matter to welcome a new business, but as with many other tricky letters, there are hidden pitfalls. Be too cool and they will think you are simply going through the motions. Be too pressing and your letter will go straight into the bin. A reasonably warm approach and a small inducement to begin a business relationship ought to do the trick.

Once again, the essentially personal nature of the letter means that is probably better not to have a heading.

2.18 A CUSTOMER WHO HAS EXCEEDED AN AGREED CREDIT LIMIT

Dear Mr Thomas

Account no. [state reference]

I note that you have exceeded your credit limit on your account [give reference].

In order to bring your balance down to the approved limit, please remit the amount of [state amount] by return.

If you are unable to do this, please contact me as soon as possible, in order to make other arrangements.

Yours sincerely

Comment

There is a temptation here to be too soft with a customer who is abusing an arrangement made. You need to be fairly formal and quite firm or the situation will continue to deteriorate. What you should not do is make threats of further action, as this may antagonise the customer and cause you to lose them as soon as they have paid off the arrears.

In that case, you would almost certainly have lost the customer for good. People do not like to feel embarrassed, even if it is all their fault.

2.19 TO A CUSTOMER PERSISTENTLY REFUSING TO PAY

Dear Mr James

Account no. [give reference]

I have written to you several times over the past three months requesting an explanation for why you have failed to bring your account with us up to date.

By ignoring these requests, you are damaging the excellent credit record you had previously maintained with our company. In addition, you are incurring additional expense to yourself and to us.

Unless I hear from you within ten days, I will have no other choice but to turn your account over for collection. I am sorry that we must take such drastic action but I am afraid you leave us no alternative. You can preserve your credit rating by remitting your cheque today for [state amount].

Yours sincerely

31

Comment

When all else fails, you have to bring the big guns to bear on the case, but the danger is that the letter will be all negative. Here, however, we praise the black sheep for his or her previous good record.

You should, though, close by stating quite clearly what you will do and by when unless you receive a favourable reply.

2.20 TO A CUSTOMER PAYING LATE FOR NO APPARENT REASON

Dear Mr Wilson

<u>Account no. [give reference]</u>

In the past 12 months you have bought a great deal of merchandise from us.

Since you have never taken advantage of the 2 per cent discount we offer for early payment, we thought that you might be unaware of just how substantial your savings could be. The savings on last year's purchases alone would have amounted to [state amount].

By paying us within 10 days of delivery, you can, over the period of a year, actually save 24 per cent of an average monthly bill. Of course, you know what is best for your own business, but we want to be sure that you are aware of this savings factor.

We would like to take this opportunity to thank you for the orders you have given to us over this past year and the promptness with which you have always paid. It is a pleasure doing business with your firm.

Yours sincerely

Comment

The tricky part in getting earlier payment out of customers, and therefore a better cash flow, is to offer some inducement. A small discount is a popular way of achieving this. The cost is likely to be outweighed by the loss of interest on money received after what may be a considerable delay, especially as many companies now expect up to 90 days in which to settle accounts.

It is worth congratulating them on their prompt payment because, with a 90 day settlement period, they will in any case regard paying at the end of that time as prompt.

2.21 GETTING ADDITIONAL BUSINESS OUT OF EXISTING CUSTOMERS

Dear Mrs Mills

Before the winter is upon us, we are recommending that our customers call us to arrange to have one of our service representatives perform a thorough and complete inspection of their heating systems.

Throughout our many years of experience we have learned that by taking certain preventative measures such as correcting a minor electrical problem, costly repairs and replacement of parts can often be avoided. Another reason we have for suggesting this inspection at this time is the fact that invariably it is during the coldest period of the winter that we are inundated with service requests. When this occurs, we are unable to provide quick service to all of our valued customers such as yourself.

Please call us so we can ensure you of a warm and comfortable winter.

Yours sincerely

Comment

I have taken the example of a heating services company for this letter, but you should be able to adapt it to any other kind of business. The tricky part is to make an offer which makes obvious sense and which the recipient, because of pressure of work, may not have had the time to consider.

It is also the kind of offer which will bring in additional work and not merely an earlier version of what you would have received in any case. Many systems, services and products will not suffer from missing the occasional service, but if you can get your customers in the habit of having regular checks, you can establish regular follow-up business to sales.

2.22 FOLLOWING UP ON SALES

Dear Ms Jennings

Thank you for leaving your business card when you paid our shop a visit. We hope you found our assortment of goods interesting. Of course, we are always purchasing new items, so we encourage you to come in and browse often.

In addition to buying from other manufacturers in Europe and in the United States, we also import from the Far East. We can, therefore, offer at all times of the year an exceptional variety of items to suit every requirement.

We look forward to seeing you soon.

Yours sincerely

Comment

The idea of maintaining a kind of visitors' book for customers is not common in business, but it is one well worth considering. You may have noticed that a number of hotels provide a jar for guests to leave their business cards. There is a draw each month and the winner receives a bottle of wine or some other inexpensive item. It provides a ready source of names and addresses for a mailshot to encourage them to do further business with you.

The difficult part is to encourage without appearing to badger.

2.23 TO A CUSTOMER WHO HAS NOT BEEN HEARD FROM FOR SOME TIME

Dear Mr Ellis

It has been so long since we have received an order from you, that I have begun to wonder if, perhaps, we have offended you in some way in the past.

If this is the case, I would greatly appreciate knowing what happened. In fact, if you have any grievance with our firm, I wish that you would call so that we might discuss the problem.

We have introduced many innovations into our product line since the last order you placed with us and if the reason we have not heard from you has nothing to do with a complaint, we would appreciate having the chance to show you these innovations.

In either case, it would be good to hear from you.

Yours sincerely

35

Comment

It is not easy to wake a 'sleeping' customer, but a personal approach might work. It may be an unvoiced complaint that has kept the customer away or it may simply be that they have not been buying anything much from anyone lately. Give them the option and invite them to contact you, but do not push too hard. This is the kind of letter you can only really send once. If it does not work, there is no point in sending it every six months or so.

2.24 TO A CUSTOMER LOSING HIS OR HER CREDIT STANDING

Dear Mr Porter

You are one of our most valued accounts and it is with deep regret that I must inform you of a change in your account credit status.

From now on, it will be necessary to send payment with each order for merchandise from your firm. We must insist upon this until your account is brought up to date, at which time we will review the position.

I know this will be an inconvenience to you and I hope that this will not interfere with our long and profitable relationship. We value your business and look forward to resolving this difficulty as soon as possible. Please call me if you wish to discuss this matter.

Yours sincerely

Comment

There can be few trickier situations to deal with in modern business than taking away someone's credit rating, but sometimes it has to be done. Your tone should be matter-of-fact and as sympathetic as it is possible to be in the circumstances. It is worth remembering that many people get into debt through no fault of their own.

It helps to soften the blow of a letter like this if you can at least offer the prospect of restoring the credit within the foreseeable future.

2.25 CUSTOMER DELAY IN RETURNING GOODS

Dear Mrs Cousins

Over the years we have had to formulate various company policies. We have never arbitrarily adopted these policies, but have chosen them in order to enable us to accommodate our customers by providing our products at the lowest conceivable prices while remaining in business.

One of these policies is that our customers have [number] days in which to return any merchandise for a full refund. We feel this allows sufficient time to inspect our products and be satisfied with their quality.

I am grateful for the business you have given our firm and am proud to have you as one of our customers. I cannot, however, authorise the return of our merchandise as you have requested, because you took delivery over [weeks] ago.

I am sorry that I cannot help you in this matter and I hope you will understand why we must take this position.

Yours sincerely

Comment

It can be useful here to set the difficulty in a general context to show that you are not discriminating against one particular customer. It also helps if you err on the generous side when fixing how much time a customer has in which to return goods they decide they do not want, for whatever reason.

The tone needs to be polite but firm. The customer has to feel that you have been reasonable and that he or she would be being unreasonable to expect you to act differently.

2.26 GUARANTEE EXPIRED ON GOODS

Dear Mr Anderson

We are sorry to hear about the problem you have had with your [name of product]. We would like to be able to make the necessary repairs at no charge to you, but, unfortunately, the guarantee has expired.

The proof of purchase you sent us shows that the product was bought on [date]. Since our guarantee is for a period of one year from the date of purchase, it expired three months ago.

If you would like us to repair the [product] for you, there will be a charge of [amount for repairs]. We will guarantee the work we do for [period of time].

Please tick the appropriate box on the enclosed instruction card and return it to us as soon as possible.

Yours sincerely

Comment

The danger here is that you will assume the customer is trying to pull a fast one. This may not be the case. They may genuinely have miscalculated how long ago they bought the product.

It is necessary to keep a cool head and explain in simple, accurate terms just what the position is. Offer to help but make it clear that there will be a charge. It is a good idea to guarantee any repairs for, say, three months. After all, if your work does not stand up for three months, should you really be in business at all?

2.27 A STRONGER APPROACH TO AN OVERDUE ACCOUNT

Dear Mr Crummock

Account no. [state reference]

Our accounts department has forwarded your overdue account to me, hoping that I can persuade you to bring it up to date before sending your file to our legal department.

When our firm extends credit to an individual such as yourself, it bases its decision on that applicant's previous credit history and ability to pay. When you requested credit from us, you met all of these criteria. Today, however, your account has reached the critical stage.

You can avoid any additional costs if you post your cheque for [amount]. I must hear from you within seven days.

Yours sincerely

39

Comment

If a stronger line is needed with a slow paying customer, you still need to remain courteous and businesslike. The temptation is to make the language stronger with the proposed action and this is a mistake. This customer will still realise that he or she must do something pretty quickly or face the consequences. Yet there is nothing particularly threatening in the language itself.

Supplies and services

3.1 ITEMS DEFECTIVE IN A DELIVERED ORDER

Dear Mrs Moore

Order no. [state reference]

We placed the following order with you on [date]:

[List items]

When the order was delivered, the following items were defective:

[List items]

Please arrange for speedy replacement of the defective items. Unless we receive them by [date] we shall be compelled to cancel the order and return items already delivered.

Yours sincerely

Comment

The main problem with this kind of letter is often lack of clarity about which items exactly are defective. It is useful, therefore, to restate exactly what you ordered and then to list the items which are defective. The heading should be specific about the reference number of the order so that the supplier can speed up checking.

Since most businesses these days only order items when they need them, time will usually be an important factor. You need to make it clear that unless the response is speedy you will have to go elsewhere for your requirements. You may even wish to strengthen the letter by stating that you will place no future orders with this supplier.

3.2 SLOW RESPONSE TO NEED FOR REPAIR

Dear Mr Lawson

Repair to [state item]

We telephoned you on [date] to report that [item] was in need of repair. This item is covered by your extended warranty which guarantees on-site attention within 24 hours.

Two days have now elapsed since we called and no one has yet been to carry out the repair. Please ensure that this matter is attended to within seven days. If the repair is not carried out within this time, we shall make arrangements ourselves to have the repair carried out and will forward the bill for this to you.

Yours sincerely

Comment

You should, of course, omit the second sentence of the first paragraph if the item is not covered by warranty or vary the wording to suit the particular kind of arrangement you have with the company who will carry out the repair.

You should be specific about both how long it is since you reported the need for repair and how long you are prepared to wait for the repairers to attend to it. If you have no warranty arrangement in being, you may wish to omit the threat to send the bill to the repairers if you have to go elsewhere for attention. However, if they have obviously accepted responsibility for repairing the item it would nevertheless be worth trying to make them pay.

3.3 UNSATISFACTORY REPAIR

Dear Mr Kelynack

Repair to [state item]

On [date] your service staff called at these premises to repair a [item]. At the end of their time here, they assured me that the [item] had been correctly repaired and then they left.

The next time I had to use the [item] at [time] on [date] I found that it was still not operating properly. The problem appears to me to be [give brief details].

I should be grateful if you would arrange for a competent person to call and assess the situation and effect the necessary repairs. I should like to be present this time to check the repair for myself. A convenient appointment for me would be [time] on [date].

42

Please telephone me immediately if this appointment is not convenient.

Yours sincerely

Comment

It is important to be quite clear about dates, items and actions in this type of letter. In the second paragraph you should beware of stating what is faulty and merely indicate what 'appears to be' faulty. It could well be that a fault may have more than one cause and, unless you are an expert, you may cause yourself more trouble if you are too positive. You should make the repairers work it out for themselves.

In the third paragraph, using the term 'competent' shows that you feel the previous repair was carried out by someone who was incompetent without your actually having to say so. Your insistence on being present when the repair is carried out tells the reader that you intend to see that the repair is done properly this time. It will not matter if you have no idea how the item works; the message will still get through that you are not happy with the way things have turned out. There is also the clear implication that future repairs had better be undertaken correctly.

3.4 REMEDYING DUPLICATION OF SUPPLY

Dear Mr Carter

Order no. [state reference]

Further to my telephone call of [date], when I spoke to [name or position held] about the duplication in the delivery of our order for [items and order no.], I should be grateful if you would resolve this problem for me.

[Name or position held] did not seem to understand that you had delivered all the items twice. He/she [select as appropriate] said that this could not happen under your system. However, the point is that it has.

Now the matter is more complicated because we have received a second bill for the goods. As we require only one set of the items, I am returning the second bill with this letter. I leave it you to arrange uplifting of the duplicate goods. If you do not arrange to recover them within 14 days, we shall make our own arrangements for their disposal.

Yours sincerely

Comment

Problems with orders may well be cleared up over the telephone, but if you do need to write you should refer to any call you have had to make. You should also ensure that you obtain a name when calling and refer to this person in the first paragraph.

The second paragraph should give any other relevant information concerning your call. If there is none, the paragraph may be omitted.

The third paragraph should state quite clearly what you intend to do with the goods and within what kind of time scale. If no second bill has been received, you should omit reference to it.

43

3.5 A LIGHT LETTER OF COMPLAINT

Dear Ms Banks

[Subject of complaint]

I was rather disappointed by the quality of your customer service on [date]. We had ordered a number of items from you and, as there seemed to be some delay in delivery, I telephoned to enquire why.

The person I spoke to, who would not give his/her [select as appropriate] name, did not seem to care very much that we were being inconvenienced by the delay. He/she [select as appropriate] simply said that this sort of thing sometimes happened and that that was all there was to it.

I feel that you should try to identify this member of your staff and point out to them the importance of the right attitude and approach when dealing with customers. Customers are, after all, the life blood of all businesses. I am sure you would not wish to lose custom simply through an offhand attitude on the part of a member of staff.

Yours sincerely

Comment

Letters of complaint come in various weights. If you are only mildly upset by what has happened, but upset enough to write, your tone should be reproachful rather than accusing. You should clearly describe the circumstances which have led to the letter.

The final paragraph should state what you expect the offending party to do about your complaint. The last sentence of the paragraph does not threaten any specific action on your part, but does contain a general warning implication.

44

3.6 A MEDIUM STRENGTH LETTER OF COMPLAINT

Dear Mrs Green

[Subject of complaint]

I was very disappointed by the quality of your customer service on [date]. We had ordered a number of items from you and delivery was late, being in excess of 28 days. This being the case, I telephoned to enquire why.

The attitude of the person I spoke to, who refused despite several requests to give his/her [select as appropriate] name, was rude and unhelpful. He/she [select as appropriate] said that I should just have to wait my turn for delivery.

This is not acceptable behaviour by anyone in business these days, as I am sure you will agree. I feel that you should identify this member of your staff and reprimand him/her. Unless his/her attitude towards customers improves, it will cost you business, the first of which could be ours. As you know, in the course of a year, we send a considerable amount of business your way. It would be a pity if the rudeness of one person were to be allowed to jeopardise this relationship.

I look forward to hearing from you that I shall not have this experience when dealing with your company in the future.

Yours sincerely

Comment

If you are more strongly miffed by the treatment you have had, you can use stronger language, but still remain courteous. One of the most common problems with letters of complaint is that writers go 'over the top' and become abusive. Very few people will respond to abuse and it may even be that your letter will go straight in the bin and be dismissed as just 'another one of those'. Clear facts and reasoned argument, expressed forcefully but not rudely, are far more likely to be effective.

45

3.7 A STRONG LETTER OF COMPLAINT

Dear Mr Chamberlain

[Subject of complaint]

I was extremely disappointed by the poor quality of your customer service on [date]. We had ordered a number of items from you and these were very late in being delivered. This delay was causing us considerable inconvenience and could have resulted in our losing business, so I telephoned to ask why the delivery was so late.

The person I spoke to was extremely rude and abusive and actually put the phone down before I could explain the full nature of our complaint. I telephoned a total of three times and the same thing happened each time.

Unless I receive a satisfactory explanation for the delay in supplying the goods within seven days you may consider the order cancelled. We shall place our future business with one of your competitors.

Yours sincerely

Comment

If you have endured really rough treatment, you can let your hair down, always remembering never to stoop to the level you have had to suffer. If you are ever as abusive or aggressive as those you complain about, you completely undermine the justness of your cause. You may, however, be quite firm about the action you propose to take if you do not receive satisfaction and be specific about when you propose to take it.

3.8 LATE DELIVERY OF GOODS

Dear Ms Stephenson

Order no. [state reference]

This order was placed with you on [date] and we were told to expect delivery within [28] days. In fact, delivery took [35] days and we think this is excessive. It could have caused us loss of business as we had to keep our own customers waiting.

We received no apology for the lateness of delivery and I feel that some form of compensation should be offered. I look forward to hearing from you on this point.

I hope that you will also ensure that all future orders are fulfilled promptly or that, if there is to be a delay, we shall be informed of this possibility immediately. We need this assurance to be able to maintain our relationship with your company.

47

Yours sincerely

Comment

This is a fairly formal business letter and as such needs a heading for ease of handling and for filing purposes.

The details should be clear and the actual figures used here should be varied according to the actual circumstances you have encountered.

The request for compensation shows the reader that you regard the situation with some seriousness. You will probably not receive any compensation, but even if you do and it only turns out to be a small business gift it will probably still be welcome.

Finally, you need to make it clear that, whilst some delays are to be expected from time to time even in the best run businesses, you want to know as soon as possible if there is going to be a problem. At no time should you allow yourself to be left in the dark. You are also quite entitled to let them know that you can place your orders elsewhere if you have to.

3.9 LETTER TO CREDITOR

Dear Mr Waistell

Account no. [state reference]

Owing to extremely difficult business conditions at the moment, we are experiencing temporary problems in maintaining payments on this account. We should very much like to secure less stringent repayment terms if possible.

I enclose a cheque for [amount] which is the maximum we are able to send at this time. I will send further payments as soon as we receive the amounts owing to us from other businesses. It is our intention that we should return to a normal repayment pattern as soon as circumstances permit.

I hope this arrangement will be acceptable to you as a short term measure, but if there are problems or you wish to discuss the matter further or require more information, please contact me personally.

Yours sincerely

Comment

Business life has its downs as well as its ups and money problems can easily arise if there is an unexpected downturn in trade. You may need to write to creditors to see if you can get a little breathing space. It is important to stress, though, that you see your difficulties as being temporary. This is a quite reasonable position to take because business by its very nature tends to be cyclical.

No matter what the hardships, it is important to offer something by way of payment and to indicate that you fully intend to return to a normal pattern as soon as possible. It is also worth making it clear that it is not your own inefficiency that has created the situation, but slow payment by those who owe you money.

The final paragraph pleads without begging and offers a direct line if the creditor wants to know more. Most creditors will be prepared to accept temporary lapses in repayment patterns since, unless they are the Inland Revenue, HM Customs & Excise, the bank or the building society, they are well down the queue if they try to squeeze too hard.

3.10 LETTER TO BUILDER ABOUT POOR WORKMANSHIP

Dear Mr Appleton

Building works at [address]

This is to confirm our telephone conversation of [date] about the works you are currently undertaking at the above address.

As I pointed out, we are not happy with the quality of workmanship in several respects. These are [briefly describe deficiencies].

We should like to have these deficiencies remedied as soon as possible and I should be grateful if you would let me know in writing within the next seven days when you will carry out this remedial work.

If I do not receive a satisfactory reply within this time, I shall be compelled to raise the matter with your trade association's customer service department.

Yours sincerely

49

Comment

You need to be formal with builders. They are often not too careful over paperwork. They are often more practically minded than other people in business. They are often better dealt with face to face.

If a letter is necessary, it should follow a meeting or telephone call. It should state the problem clearly and simply.

You should make it clear that you want action and the deadline by which that action is to be completed.

Finally, you need to be prepared to take matters further if the matter is not put right. The next best step with a builder is probably whichever trade association he or she belongs to.

3.11 UNRELIABLE SUPPLIER

Dear Mr Blair

Account no. [state reference]

Over the last few months, I have had to complain to you several times about late and incomplete deliveries of orders. These problems have begun to cause us embarrassing difficulties with some of our own customers and the matter clearly needs to be resolved.

I can see no reason why normal standards of business efficiency and customer care cannot be maintained by you and I look forward to hearing that you have taken steps to ensure prompt and complete deliveries in future.

Unless you are able to assure me that this will be the case, we shall have no alternative but to place our business with one of your competitors. Because of the long standing nature of our relationship, I should be most reluctant to do this, but it may become inevitable unless matters improve by the end of next month.

Yours sincerely

Comment

Some degree of formality and a firm tone are necessary here. It is no good being mild and polite in the hope that the offending party will mend his or her ways. A direct 'I – you' viewpoint is preferable, so that the recipient knows straight away that he or she is dealing with someone who has had enough and now wants some action.

If there are only a few instances of unreliability, it can be useful to list and briefly describe them. This letter, however, assumes that there has been a general deterioration and that there are really too many complaints to list. It further assumes that there are not so many over so long a period that it is too late to be complaining.

A finish on a deadline will tell the reader that you are serious both about your complaints and about what you will do if they are not speedily attended to.

3.12 LETTER CONTAINING A CONTRACT TO SUPPLY A SERVICE

Dear Mrs Wright

Supply of [state service]

Further to our telephone discussions held over recent days, I am now able to commission you to perform [state service details].

This will be subject to our normal conditions for such services, two copies of which I enclose. I should be grateful if you would sign one of these, as indication of your acceptance of the terms, and return it to me as soon as possible.

I look forward to working with you and to a highly successful completion of [state service].

Yours sincerely

Contract to supply [state service]

1 This Agreement is made between [you] ('the Company') and [the service provider] ('the Contractor').

2 The Company requires the Contractor to provide [brief description of service].

3 This Agreement shall take effect on signature and shall be completed by [date].

4 The terms of the Agreement may only be varied by the written mutual consent of both parties.

5 Nothing in this Agreement shall be taken to constitute a Contract of Employment nor is it the intention of either yourselves or the Company that you shall be employees of the Company.

6 The daily fee for your services on the days you are required to provide them and do so will be [amount], excluding VAT.

7 During the currency of this Agreement the Contractor shall be responsible for ensuring that:

7.1 The Contractor and anyone acting on his behalf shall not commit an act of discrimination rendered unlawful by the Sex Discrimination Act 1975 or the Race Relations Act 1976 or any enactment supplementing or modifying the same.

7.2 All necessary steps are taken to ensure the health, safety and welfare of the Contractor's staff within the applicable requirements of the Health and Safety at Work Act 1974 and any enactment supplementing or modifying the same.

8 It is a condition of this Contract that you agree to be bound by the terms of the Company's Secrecy Agreement, a copy of which can be obtained from the Company.

9 Copyright in any materials produced in connection with this Agreement shall rest in the Company.

10 This Agreement may be terminated by either party giving to the other one month's written notice without cause assigned.

11 In the event of a material breach of this Agreement either party reserves the right at any time to serve on the party in breach a notice in writing to terminate this Agreement instantly.

12 The validity, construction and performance of this Agreement shall be governed by English Law.

Authorised to sign for and on behalf of the Company:
Signature:
Name:
Date:

Authorised to sign for and on behalf of the Contractor:
Signature:
Name:
Date:

Comment

Letters like this can be tricky because you have to ensure that the contract covers all the matters that need to be covered. The example given here covers some of the main points that most contracts will cover, but there may well be items you can delete because they do not apply to the situation you are dealing with. Similarly, there may be additional items to be included.

Such a letter would normally follow telephone or face-to-face discussions and may be little more than a formality. But formalities can become important when things go wrong, so it is necessary to get them right.

3.13 LETTER TO BUS COMPANY SEEKING IMPROVEMENTS IN SERVICES

Dear Sirs

Service [give name and number]

Many of our employees rely upon this service to get them to work in the morning and to return them home at night. Recently, however, this service has become unreliable and we have received a number of complaints about buses running late or even failing to turn up altogether. I enclose a list of the complaints we have received [attach this to letter].

We are an important provider of employment in this area and have many customers who depend on us for the products/services [select as appropriate] we provide. If our employees are late for work, we lose valuable production time. This can mean that our service to our customers is impaired and this further means that their efficiency is adversely affected. A reliable public transport service is therefore essential not only to us but to other members of this community.

I should be most grateful if you would investigate these complaints and let me know what you propose to do to ensure that the service is more reliable in future.

Yours faithfully

Complaints (examples) about service [name and number]

1 Buses are often full.

2 Buses have not been properly cleaned and are dirty and untidy.

3 Long queues build up at certain popular stops and bus shelters are too small.

4 Buses often run late.

5 Buses often do not turn up at all.

6 Drivers are surly and unhelpful.

7 Many buses are old and keep breaking down.

53

8 Timetables at bus stops are inadequate and confusing and printed in a typeface which is too small.

9 There are no seats at bus stops.

10 There are too few inspectors to check that everybody has bought a ticket.

11 Many people have to wait for long periods when they have to catch connecting services.

12 There appears to be no way of informing passengers when buses are running late.

13 Heating on the buses is often not turned on in winter.

14 Some buses make unscheduled stops or the route is changed for no apparent reason.

15 Bus fares are too high for the quality of service provided.

16 Seats are uncomfortable and there is too little space between rows.

17 Some drivers leave early to avoid picking people up when they leave work at the end of the afternoon.

18 Some drivers do not attempt to drive smoothly when they have standing passengers.

19 There is inadequate space for storing shopping and other items.

20 Several people have already complained but received no reply.

Comment

It is very tempting with this kind of letter of complaint to be abusive. You are, after all, only dealing with the local bus company who may have been around for so long they are almost like a wayward member of the family. Resist the temptation. It is quite possible that you need them more than they need you. Bus routes can be changed.

A reasoned and reasonable plea for co-operation in both your interests is perhaps the best approach. Plenty of facts and sound arguments will underline the fact that an improvement will help everybody.

Do not set a deadline for a reply, but encourage them to move with some speed. This they are more likely to do if they feel they are dealing with a sensible person who wants to help them as much as himself or herself.

3.14 LETTER TO ELECTRICITY COMPANY COMPLAINING ABOUT AN INACCURATE METER READING

Dear Sirs

Inaccurate meter reading

When we received your bill for the last quarter, we found that it was inaccurate in the following respects:

[List inaccuracies]

Our own calculations show that the amount due to you is [amount].

I should be grateful if you would investigate these apparent discrepancies and then send us a revised bill for payment.

If there is any further information you require, please contact me personally.

Yours faithfully

Comment

In this kind of letter it is important to be as specific as possible because it is often not possible to identify precisely the member of staff who will deal with it.

A list will help the person at the other end to check that all of your complaints have been attended to. It will also help you to check that all necessary actions have been taken.

Even though it may be impossible to know who will deal with the letter, you can at least ensure that if they have any queries they can approach a specific person at your end.

c

3.15 LETTER TO GAS COMPANY ABOUT DEFECTIVE SERVICING

Dear Sirs

Defective servicing

On [date] your engineer called at these offices to service [details of equipment]. When he left, the equipment appeared to be functioning normally. However, within [duration] of his leaving the following fault/s occurred/recurred [select as appropriate]:

[Details of faults]

We have made temporary arrangements to be able to operate without this equipment, but we clearly need to have it working properly as soon as possible.

I should be grateful, therefore, if you would arrange for an engineer to call on [date] when I shall be able to check personally on completion of the work.

Yours faithfully

Comment

Again, it may be difficult to find out who will deal with the letter, so you need to be as specific as possible and to show that you are giving this matter your personal attention.

In setting a date for an engineer to call, you need to bear in mind that not all letters reach their destinations the following day, especially now that more and more businesses are using second class post to save costs.

3.16 LETTER TO WATER COMPANY ABOUT BREAK IN SUPPLY

Dear Sirs

<u>Break in supply</u>

Further to my telephone conversation today with a member of your customer service staff, I am writing to confirm my complaint about a break in the supply of water to these premises of [duration] on [date].

Though we do not rely on water supply for our products/services [select as appropriate], we do rely on it for the comfort and convenience of staff, hygiene and so on. It is most inconvenient therefore to experience an unheralded break in supply.

I should be grateful if you will investigate the circumstances of the break, report them to me and ensure that if similar breaks occur in future we receive as much notice as can reasonably be given.

Yours faithfully

57

Comment

Breaks in water supply seem to be happening with increasing frequency as ageing water mains become less reliable. It might therefore be useful to have a standard letter ready to hand should this happen to your business.

You need to be specific about the duration of the break in service and the date on which it occurred. Again, it is necessary to avoid the temptation to be abusive.

You also need to ensure that the reply comes direct to you and does not get lost in the general mail.

3.17 LETTER TO BRITISH TELECOM ABOUT EXCESSIVE BILL

Dear Sirs

Telephone bill for the period [give details]

We have just received our bill for [period in question] and were surprised to find that it was as high as it was.

Upon examining it in detail, we find a number of calls charged which could not possibly have been made from this number. These calls were as follows:

[List details of calls]

You will notice that these include several international calls. You have yourselves installed equipment here to prevent these and other unauthorised calls being made.

I shall be grateful therefore if you will investigate these inaccuracies and send us an amended bill for payment.

Yours faithfully

Comment

Errors in telephone bills seem to be becoming more frequent and people find they are charged for calls they could not possibly have made. It is always tricky when dealing with former public corporations over matters like this. Privatisation has not made all staff as customer oriented as they should be.

Be firm, be specific and be sure of your ground. Let them prove that the bill should be as high as it is.

3.18 REJECTING GOODS THAT ARE NOT LIKE THE SAMPLES PROVIDED

Dear Mrs Arnott

Order no. [give number]

Before we placed this order with you, you provided us with samples of the items in which we had expressed interest. These samples were of a type and quality which appeared to meet our requirements. It was on the basis of this that we placed the order.

When we took delivery of the goods, inspection showed that the items delivered were not of the same quality as the samples. There were also several significant deviations from the specifications of the samples.

We feel that, in the circumstances, unless you are able to deliver our order with items which match the samples, we have no alternative but to cancel the order, return the goods and seek another source of supply. Please let me know within seven days whether you are able to supply the goods on these terms. If you cannot, please let me know what arrangements you have made to collect the unsuitable items.

Yours sincerely

Comment

This could be a tricky situation if there is any possibility of the response being that the samples were only intended to indicate in general terms the nature and quality of the goods. This letter assumes that you were specifically told that the goods would match the samples. If you were not, then you should make sure that next time you are.

The tone should be businesslike and fairly formal. You need to give the clear impression that you have not received fair treatment. In this way, it becomes more likely that the supplier will suddenly 'find' the goods you should have had in the first place. It would not be the first time that someone had assumed that the main delivery would not be checked quite so thoroughly as the samples. Samples after all are often examined by those who make the purchasing decisions; deliveries are often handled by staff who are well down the chain of command.

3.19 REQUESTING MORE TIME TO PAY IN AN UNEXPECTED EMERGENCY

Dear Ms Roberts

My next payment will be due on [date].

Due to an unexpected emergency that has occurred, I will be unable to make this payment by the [date]. I am therefore requesting an extension of [duration] to make this payment.

If you review my file, I believe you will find that my payments have generally been made on time. My relationship with your company is very important to me, as well as my desire to maintain a good credit rating.

I hope you will feel able to consider this request sympathetically.

Yours sincerely

Comment

It is never easy asking for time to pay, but it is sometimes necessary. The difficult part is in deciding how far to grovel before your creditors. It is best to be positive and to propose a definite alternative method of paying. There is always the old adage about people only giving credit to those who do not need it to be borne in mind.

3.20 MAKING INSTRUCTIONS CLEAR

Dear Mrs Kimberley

I have received confirmation from [name of company] that they are to proceed with their [title] conference for a group of their junior managers at your hotel from 27 October 199– to 3 November 199–. I hope you have also received the booking forms from them.

We shall require the following facilities for the conference and I should be most grateful if you would arrange to provide them and put them on the [name of company] account where necessary:

A seminar room capable of accommodating 14 people in space and comfort (about 24 people for one or two of the sessions)

Two syndicate rooms capable of accommodating about four people each

In the seminar room:

Flipchart
Overhead projector and screen
Video camera, recorder and monitor (this is the most important item of equipment required)

In the syndicate rooms:

Flipchart

Transport between the hotel and Newcastle Airport [change as appropriate] at the start and end of the visit will be required. I am told the party will be flying into Newcastle at about 5.30 p.m. on the 27th, but I shall receive confirmation of the flight number and precise time of arrival nearer the date.

[Name of company] will also require the use of an executive style coach capable of seating up to about 18 people, or possibly a few more, in some comfort for several of the sessions for visits and tours. At the moment, the likely times are Sunday afternoon, Tuesday evening to visit a theatre in Sunderland or Newcastle [change as appropriate], Wednesday afternoon and evening, Thursday afternoon and evening and Friday morning and afternoon.

We intend to take them on a familiarisation tour of the region on Sunday afternoon. Would you be able to arrange for the Tourist Board or someone else to provide a suitable guide?

[Name of company] wish to hold a welcoming dinner for themselves and four local managers (aged about 30–35) with their partners on the Sunday evening. Do you have contact with any local organisation able to suggest suitable names for invitation? As there is one lady in the group, the presence of at least one lady manager would be an advantage.

Do you have contact with any organisation able to provide a speaker on the regional economy for the morning of the 28th, starting at about 10.30 a.m. and speaking for about an hour, including questions?

Do you have any contacts in local universities who may be able to invite the group to a lecture one evening? A [type of department] or similar department would seem to be most appropriate as [name of company] is a [nature of business] company.

They are also interested in gaining access to the following facilities at some time during the visit: golf (+ trainer), swimming, indoor tennis, walking, horse riding and squash. Not everyone is interested in all of these activities, so they could be offered simultaneously for personal preference if necessary. Would you have contacts with any places able to help provide these?

If there are any of the above facilities which you are not able to provide, do let me know and I will contact other sources of assistance.

Please let me know if you require any further information. I shall be away from home conducting seminars every day this week, but I shall be at home in the evenings and the answerphone will be on during the day for messages. I could visit the hotel any evening if there are matters which you wish to discuss in person. I shall be in Jersey on business from 22 October until 25 October. I shall be free on 26 October to deal with any last minute arrangements.

Best wishes,

Yours sincerely

Comment

I have chosen a specific example from personal experience here because I think it shows the need to be especially careful with both language and layout when giving instructions. Ideally, it should be so arranged that the recipient can tick off the items as they have done them.

You will need to vary the details to suit your particular requirements.

3.21 REJECTING A CLAIM FOR PAYMENT

Dear Mr Wallis

Invoice no. [state reference]

We have received this invoice which is your claim for payment for [state service].

I have made enquiries and I understand that you have not, in fact, provided the full services we requested. Specifically, you have failed to [briefly describe deficiencies].

In the light of these deficiencies, I regret that I cannot authorise payment of your invoice. If you will supply me with evidence that you have remedied the deficiencies, I shall then authorise payment.

If you wish to discuss this matter, please contact me personally.

Yours sincerely

Comment

This has to be a formal letter. Someone has let you down and you have to be quite firm with them. You have to be quite specific about what they have failed to do. You then have to make quite clear what you intend to do in response.

If it is possible for them to remedy their failings, you should give them this opportunity. You should also give them the chance to put their case to you in person. If you are in the right, and you need to make sure that you are, you have nothing to fear from this.

4

Sub-contractors

4.1 WORK NOT DONE TO STANDARD AGREED

Dear Mr Allen

Items of work requiring further attention

At our meeting on [date], we discussed the following items of work undertaken by you which did not at that time meet expected and promised standards:

[Numbered descriptive list of items]

I have today toured the site with [name of accompanying person and position held] and we have found that on items [insert numbers from above list] the work still does not meet the necessary standard.

You are aware that, under the terms of our contract, we would be quite entitled at this point to invoke Clause [insert number of relevant penalty clause]. We would, however, prefer not to do this if you will undertake to ensure that the work is completed to the level agreed within [specify number] days.

Please let me know by return if this will not be possible.

Yours sincerely

Comment

The problems with this type of letter are: it is not made clear to the sub-contractor exactly what needs to be done; the sub-contractor needs to be clear that you are firm in your intention to secure action; you need to avoid threatening in such a way that the sub-contractor digs his or her heels in.

The best way to overcome these problems is to use numbered lists for ease of reference, to make it clear that legal means can be used but are not yet being implemented and to write in a polite but firm tone. It also helps to indicate clearly the deadline for any response, in this case 'by return'.

4.2 CONFIRMING WHAT HAS BEEN AGREED AT A MEETING

Dear Mr Slater

Confirmation of matters agreed at meeting on [date]

At the meeting between [organisation or group of people sending the letter] and [organisation or group of people receiving the letter] on [date] at [time] held at [location], we agreed the following items:

[Number and list concisely the matters agreed, for example:

1 You would provide us with regular monthly reports on the progress of the project;

2 You would invoice us for your fees and expenses covered by our agreement at monthly intervals;

3 We would inspect the work regularly to assure ourselves that it was being completed to the standards agreed;

4 We would pay invoices promptly upon receipt;

5 You would replace any personnel we felt were not performing to the standard agreed with mutually acceptable personnel;

6 Either party could call a joint meeting at any time if unforeseen problems arose and needed to be resolved.]

If you feel there are any inaccuracies or omissions in this list of items agreed, please contact me personally as soon as possible.

Yours sincerely

Comment

Everybody who attends a meeting leaves it with their own ideas about what has been agreed. For this reason, it is particularly important to send the letter confirming agreement as soon as possible after the event and certainly within 48 hours. If you leave it longer than this, there is an increased chance that people's memories of what actually happened will have changed.

It is useful to list items rather than write in paragraphs. This helps readers to check off points one at a time and reduces the risk that they will overlook something or misread it. You do need to remember that many people are quite slow readers and, when tested, do not fully understand what they have read. A typical reading speed for the average manager is about 200–250 words a minute with a 75 per cent comprehension level. This speed compares with a speaking speed of 150–180 words per minute.

You should end by giving the reader the opportunity to come back to you if they do not accept your list of items agreed. Too many writers try to avoid having to do this if they can.

4.3 TENTATIVE INVITATION TO TENDER

Dear Ms Searle

[Title of Project]

We are considering beginning work on this project in the near future, though at this stage our intentions are not fixed. The final decision on whether or not to proceed will depend on a number of factors, one of which is receipt of a suitable tender for the work.

Bearing in mind the provisional nature of this invitation to tender, we should like to know if you would be interested in tendering for the work. It would also be helpful to us if you could provide us with as much detail as is possible in such a tentative venture. An indication of the likely global figure that you might require would be useful in enabling us to decide whether or not we should wish to proceed with the project.

If you require any further information, please contact me personally.

Yours sincerely

Comment

Since the decision on whether or not to go ahead has not yet been made, the tone here needs to be less positive and more tentative. You need to avoid committing yourself too far whilst at the same time being sufficiently encouraging for people to respond.

The reader may well need more than one reminder of the provisional nature of the project. This should be followed by requests for detail and broad costs, so that the reader is left with the impression that, if the figures add up, there is a good chance of the project going ahead.

It is perhaps even more important than it usually is that the reader is given a personal contact to approach if he or she requires more information or advice.

4.4 SEEKING CHANGE OF PERSONNEL ON A PROJECT

Dear Mrs Gibson

[Title of project]

Further to our telephone conversations about our unhappiness at the quality of work produced by certain personnel, I should be grateful if, within the terms of our agreement, you would arrange to replace the following people:

[List names and positions held]

I very much regret having to ask for this step to be taken, but, as you know, we have made our misgivings very clear at recent meetings between ourselves when we have discussed the standards of performance achieved by certain members of your staff. We feel that the deficiencies cannot be made up in the time available to us by alternative methods, such as training or closer supervision. It has become necessary, therefore, to invoke the terms of our agreement and seek the changes I have described.

I look forward to seeing an early implementation of these changes and a consequent improvement in performance.

Yours sincerely

Comment

This kind of letter should always be preceded by face to face discussions. It is the kind of letter which, since it deals with people, should contain no surprises. Its purpose is really to confirm something that you have already agreed with the other people involved.

There is no need to commit to paper the precise reasons why the performance of the people named falls below expected standards. These will have emerged during the discussions and the reader will be well aware of them.

4.5 SLOW PROGRESS ON WORK OF OTHERWISE GOOD QUALITY

Dear Ms Leach

[Title of project]

Further to our discussions at recent meetings about the rate of progress on this project, I have now become so concerned at the slowness of this progress that I feel action needs to be taken.

I must emphasise that we are in no way dissatisfied at the quality of the work being produced, only at the speed of progress. The project should have reached a much more advanced stage by now and I am concerned that, unless the rate of progress increases substantially very soon, we shall see an unacceptable rise in costs.

I should be grateful, therefore, if you would let me have your proposals within the next seven days for increasing the speed of work.

Yours sincerely

69

Comment

The best laid plans do not always work out smoothly and, from time to time, it is necessary to apply the whip. You should always do this as lightly as possible and yet with sufficient firmness to provoke a reaction.

Praise where you can. Express disappointment rather than anger. Prompt the reader to take action. If this does not work, then, as with letters of complaint, the tone can stiffen and the language can become stronger until you receive a satisfactory response.

4.6 REJECTING A TENDER

Dear Mr Parker

[Title of project tendered for]

Thank you very much for your tender for this project, which we received on [date].

I regret that I have to inform you that, on this occasion, your tender has not been successful. Whilst it met the specifications required, we have awarded the contract to another tenderer who also met the specifications, but was able to do this at a lower total cost.

We expect that we shall be inviting tenders for other projects in the future and hope that you will feel able to submit for those which are of interest to you.

Yours sincerely

Comment

When you have to let people down, it helps if you can let them down lightly. If they have not succeeded, there is no need to rub salt in by an uncaring tone and style.

You cannot avoid telling them they have not won the tender, so it is as well to get this out of the way quickly. You can then build them up a little by making it appear that they have not failed hopelessly. It is just that you had to make a decision and on this occasion it did not go their way.

You might also point out that there will be other opportunities for them to consider.

4.7 CHANGE OF MIND ABOUT WORK REQUIRED

Dear Mr Shelley

[Title of Contract]

As you know, as part of this contract, you were sub-contracted to provide [indicate nature of goods or services to be provided]. I should like you to know that we have been very pleased with the standard of work produced by your staff.

However, it has, unfortunately, become necessary to change some of the goods/services [specify as appropriate] you have provided. The reasons for these changes are [give these briefly].

In future, what we shall require will be [give brief details].

I am very sorry this has become necessary. I can assure you that it is not something that we were able to foresee at the beginning of the project. I do hope that you can adapt to the new requirements without too much inconvenience.

If there are any difficulties in achieving this, please contact me personally without delay so that we can discuss possible solutions. We should very much like to keep you involved in the project.

Yours sincerely

Comment

Plans can always go wrong and when they do it is best to be open and above-board about it. Praise what has been done so far.

Explain the reasons for the changes. Apologise. Try to keep them involved. You can do little more.

You might perhaps offer to meet and discuss any difficulties with them. This would be a more effective method of tackling any problems.

4.8 COMPLAINT ABOUT QUALITY OF MATERIALS USED

Dear Mr Welsh

Materials used on [details of job]

I have inspected the work done so far on [job] and am concerned to note that the quality of the materials being used does not appear to match the specification we agreed.

I should be grateful if you would investigate this matter and let me have a report within seven days.

If, indeed, the materials being used are different in any way from those agreed, I should like a full explanation of how this occurred. I should also like to know what you propose to do to rectify the situation.

Yours sincerely

Comment

It always presents certain difficulties if sub-contractors try to cut corners in the hope of saving a little (or even a lot) on costs and it is a matter which needs handling with some care.

If the approach is too aggressive, it may provoke a digging in of heels. If it is too light-handed, it may be ignored.

You should make it clear that you expect the matter to be taken seriously and that there should be appropriate action to remedy the situation. A positive businesslike tone will help to convey the seriousness with which you view the situation.

4.9 COMPLAINT ABOUT BREAKS TAKEN BY STAFF

Dear Mr Ayre

Staff's breaks

I have noted on several occasions in the last month that the frequency and duration of the tea and lunch breaks taken by your staff have increased. This has now reached a point where it is slowing down the progress of the work significantly.

Specifically, I have recorded the following instances:

[Give brief, detailed list of breaks and their durations and numbers of staff involved]

Please investigate this matter for yourself and then let me know in writing what actions you propose to take to ensure that the pattern of breaks is restored to a reasonable level.

Please also let me know how the backlog of work will be made up so that the project is back on schedule.

Yours sincerely

73

Comment

This is a sensitive situation in which you really do need to be sure of your facts. There are few things more sacrosanct to the worker than tea and lunch breaks, so you do need a full and accurate record of any transgressions from the permitted limits.

It is useful to have your data checked by the sub-contractor as well, so that any action taken has the support of both of you. You are entitled to throw the onus for action on to the sub-contractor because they are responsible for their own staff. You also want to make sure that any shortfall in performance is made up as quickly as possible.

4.10 WORK NOT DONE AT ALL

Dear Mr Craggs

<u>Omissions from work programme</u>

On examining the records of work done in the last month, I find that there has been no progress at all on [briefly describe area or aspect omitted].

I am very concerned that this should have happened and that you have departed from the agreed programme without consultation. This work is an integral part of the total project and must be completed as soon as possible.

Please let me have your proposals in writing for undertaking the work within the next seven days. If this is not possible, please contact me immediately.

Yours sincerely

Comment

You need to be quite specific about the area of neglect and to express concern that the sub-contractors have made unauthorised changes to the programme. This clearly should not have happened.

You should indicate the urgency for action and the importance of a response by setting a tight deadline and asking for a response in writing. The guilty party has to realise that you will not tolerate such unauthorised departures from your agreement.

You should use a fairly formal businesslike approach and avoid any emotive language which might well convey your annoyance, but which might produce negative responses in the mind of the reader. This is another situation in which you do not want them to dig their heels in.

Explosions of anger are all too easy in this kind of case. That is why it is probably better to write in the first instance rather than seek a face to face confrontation. This both underlines the seriousness of the situation and gives you time to cool down before trying to resolve matters.

Agents and distributors

5.1 AGENTS AND DISTRIBUTORS SEEKING GREATER EFFORTS

Dear Mr Davison

As you know, we are always very appreciative of the efforts you make on our behalf in securing mutually profitable business within your territory. In the past, we have both benefited greatly from your work.

It is, therefore, with a little concern that I note, on checking the returns for the last period [this may be specified], that results are not as good as for the same period last year. I understand that trading conditions are not easy. In fact, because of the competitive nature of our business, they rarely are.

I do feel, however, that this may be a good time to review our market strategy to see if we can identify ways of improving upon results. To that end, I should be grateful if you would let me have your proposals for increasing our share of the available business. There may well be things that both of us could do to render a difficult situation a little more productive. For this reason, you may well wish to suggest not only what you can do to assist, but also what we might do by way of additional cost effective support.

I look forward to hearing from you very soon.

Best wishes,

Yours sincerely

Comment

Even though this letter is seeking to generate improved performance, it will be more effective if it uses the carrot rather than the stick. If people are already trying their best to succeed, a recriminatory tone will not result in a positive response.

Begin with praise. Follow this with disappointment. End with a positive suggestion that will focus everyone's attention on the light at the end of the tunnel rather than on the tunnel you are all currently in.

The 'Best wishes' reinforces the point that we need to work together on this problem.

5.2 OVERSEAS AGENT NOT PERFORMING AS EXPECTED

Dear Mr Herdman

You will recall that, when we entered the agreement to use your services as one of our agents/distributors [specify as appropriate], we set certain targets for achievement. We fully expected that, whilst these might not be met immediately, we should by now be close to achieving them, if not actually beating them.

It is a little disappointing, then, to note from the latest returns that there is a gap between targets and performance. We should like to do everything we can to close this gap.

I should be grateful, therefore, if you would let me know as soon as possible what you propose to do to achieve the agreed targets.

Yours sincerely

Comment

This letter assumes that the overseas agent may well be someone whose first language is not English. In this situation it is particularly important to keep the language as simple and clear as possible to avoid the danger of misunderstandings or of causing unintended offence. Some cultures around the world are especially sensitive to criticism, seeing in it a loss of face.

You can express disappointment, but then you need to adopt a co-operative stance. You will solve the problem together.

You end by asking what contribution they can make. They, after all, are the people in the field and they should be able to see more clearly than you can from a distance what they should do.

5.3 AGENT WHO IS NOT COMPLYING WITH TERMS OF AGREEMENT

Dear Mr Magee

Agreement between [your company] and [agent]

I note with regret, from the information you have supplied, that it is clear you are not operating within the terms of the agreement we made between us.

Specifically, I would draw your attention to the following areas within which the agreement is not being followed:

[List discrepancies between agreement and actual performance]

I feel I must insist that in the future you do comply with our agreement. As you know, we both have the right to terminate the agreement at any time if either party is not adhering to it. Rather than do this, I should like to receive your written assurance that you will keep to the terms agreed.

Yours sincerely

Comment

Where things are clearly going wrong, it is best to face the problem head on. The tone and style should be more formal. Once again, since the first language of the agent may not be English, you need to be clear and direct. Even if the agent is an English speaker, a situation where things have gone wrong is best approached with as little circumlocution as possible. The more complex the language you use, the greater the danger the reader may wriggle out of a commitment by replying in rather vague terms. This is less easy to do if your initial approach is straightforward and businesslike.

The last paragraph lays down specifically how the reader must respond if they are to satisfy you that they will abide by your agreement in future.

5.4 AGENT/DISTRIBUTOR OBTAINING BUSINESS OUTSIDE OWN TERRITORY

Dear Mr Oliver

As you know, when we appointed you as our agent/distributor [specify as appropriate], we agreed that your territory should be [briefly describe territory]. We both felt that this would provide sustainable business opportunities for the company.

I note though, from your latest returns, that some items have been obtained from other territories. Whilst we are always happy to receive business from any source, I feel it is unfair on the appointed agents/distributors [specify] for those territories for you to seek business within them.

In future, I should be grateful if you would consult me personally before approaching customers/clients [specify] who are more appropriately the concern of other agents. If you feel that your area no longer provides sufficient opportunities for business, perhaps this is something we should discuss.

I look forward to hearing from you as soon as possible.

Yours sincerely

Comment

No one wants to turn away business, so it is quite likely here that you are not too upset that someone is not quite abiding by the rules. Results are after all what counts. But if their actions are going to upset others whom you do not wish to upset, then you have to act.

The offer of a face to face discussion is a way of calling them into your office without making it sound as if the headmaster wants to see them. It is not necessary with this kind of letter to set a deadline for a reply. You can always follow it up if they have not responded within a reasonable amount of time.

The 'I – you' viewpoint is important in establishing a co-operative tone and a feeling that you can solve the problem if you both work together.

5.5 DISPUTING AGENT'S/DISTRIBUTOR'S COMMISSION CLAIMS

Dear Mr Robinson

Commission claims for [state period]

Thank you for your commission claim for the period [give dates].

Upon examining it, I note that there are certain orders which have not been placed in accordance with our normal procedures. In some cases, orders were incorrect and in others they were not clear as to exactly what was required by the customer.

Specifically, the problems were as follows:

[Briefly describe problems]

This has all led to additional work in the office for our own staff to such an extent that the costs of such work have become a significant problem. I should be grateful, therefore, if in future you would submit orders clearly and in the correct format.

If you have any difficulty in achieving this, please contact me personally.

Yours sincerely

Comment

This is a formal letter and needs a heading. The facts need to be stated clearly and concisely. It has to be clear that this person is causing extra work for other people in the organisation and that this must cease. It is therefore almost disciplinary in tone as it must make it obvious that matters cannot continue in this way.

It should, however, end with an offer of help if there are problems at the other end. It is possible that, if the agent or distributor is not English, there is simply a language difficulty which needs to be overcome, perhaps by simplifying procedures.

5.6 AGENT NOT PRODUCING BUSINESS

Dear Mr Smurthwaite

I was most concerned when I read your last report, which we received on [date], that you do not appear to have produced any new business at all in the last month/quarter [specify as appropriate].

It is always difficult at the best of times, I know, to generate new business in highly competitive conditions. We do. however, need to see an improvement in the position in the next month/quarter [specify].

I should be most grateful if you would let me know as soon as possible what new initiatives you feel you can take to improve the prospects of securing new business. If there is anything which you feel we on our part can do to assist you, please let me have details.

Yours sincerely

81

Comment

It always presents a tricky situation when someone is not performing as expected. Do you cut your losses straight away and try someone else? Or do you give them another chance? This letter supposes that you have decided to give them this other chance.

Its tone needs to be less formal and more personal, so a heading may not be needed. You should convey the impression that you are still partners working together. Nevertheless, you should make it clear that you do expect the agent to do something, by working harder on your behalf or by trying new approaches.

It is perhaps best not to give a deadline for the response, but you would probably follow the letter with a telephone call within the week to see what the agent proposed to do. You might even have some suggestions of your own by then, perhaps after discussions with colleagues.

5.7 AGENT WORKING FOR A COMPETITOR AS WELL

Dear Mr Vickers

Breach of contract

I was surprised to discover from a chance encounter with one of our competitors, [name], that you have produced business for them as well as ourselves.

This is clearly a breach of our agreement and I would like your written assurance that this practice will cease forthwith.

If you feel that you cannot give this undertaking, I shall have to terminate our agreement, under the provisions of Clause [state number].

Please let me have your reply within 14 days.

Yours sincerely

Comment

Some people find this a difficult problem to deal with, especially if they have developed a close working relationship with the agent. If, however, they have clearly breached their contract then you have to take some form of firm action.

You should use a formal approach and quasi-legal language to make your intention to resolve the matter quite obvious. You cannot let a situation like this continue.

For this reason, you should set a reasonable, but fairly tight, deadline by which you expect a reply.

5.8 DISTRIBUTOR MAINTAINING INSUFFICIENT STOCKS

Dear Mrs Winter

Stock levels

We have received a number of complaints from customers that they have not been able to obtain certain items from you because they were out of stock.

As you know, our agreement is that you shall maintain in your warehouse adequate stock for reasonable levels of demand. This clearly is not happening.

We expect you to remedy the situation as soon as possible and we shall co-operate in seeing to it that you receive an adequate supply of relevant items within [number] days of receiving your order.

If you have any difficulty in complying with our agreement, please contact me immediately as we may have to consider alternative courses of action.

83

Yours sincerely

Comment

Many people would be inclined to deal with this kind of problem by means of a telephone call. The trouble with that is that, unless you are in the habit of recording all calls, you have no record that you have done anything. It is far better, and less distasteful than recording calls, to write and make it clear what you expect the distributor to do.

There could be many reasons, of course, why adequate stocks are not being maintained – lack of space; the delay is actually at your end; they have adopted a policy of 'just-in-time' or only carrying enough stocks for immediate needs. A more worrying possibility is that they are becoming insolvent. In this case, you will wish to know this in time to remove whatever stocks they do have of yours before a liquidator comes in and freezes everything.

5.9 DISTRIBUTOR LOSING TOO MUCH BY THEFT

Dear Ms Almond

Shrinkage levels

I note, from comparing your orders from us with actual sales, that there is a high level of shrinkage at your warehouse. I have made enquiries and I understand that this is due to a number of break-ins and consequent thefts.

Clearly, we cannot allow this to continue. We both need to take the necessary action to feel that we are operating on a more secure basis.

I should be grateful if you would let me know what action you propose to take to make your premises more secure and to reduce the number of thefts.

Yours sincerely

Comment

You should use a formal approach here to underline the seriousness of the situation and your determination that the distributor should resolve it and resolve it quickly.

You need to take a positive approach and look to the future. There is little point in crying over spilt milk. The main thing is to make sure that matters improve and improve as soon as possible.

Since it is their responsibility to secure their premises, not just to protect your goods, but to ensure that their insurers will continue to insure them, there is no need for you to offer to get involved. You should place the onus firmly on them.

5.10 DISTRIBUTOR DAMAGING GOODS BY CARELESSNESS

Dear Mr Burnett

Damaged goods

I have noted from your records of goods received from us and those subsequently sold to customers that an unacceptable number of items receive damage.

We cannot continue to support this level of damage and accordingly would ask that you take whatever steps are necessary to improve the situation immediately.

Please let me know as soon as possible what action you have taken to ensure more careful handling of goods in the future.

Yours sincerely

85

Comment

There could be many reasons why goods are damaged, not the least of which might be that it makes them easier to steal without anyone worrying too much where they have gone. They were damaged, after all, weren't they?

Rather than simply telephoning about the matter, it will be useful to have something in fairly firm terms in writing.

Again the responsibility is theirs for taking action, but you should insist on knowing what it is they propose to do.

5.11 DISTRIBUTOR NOT MAINTAINING ADEQUATE RECORDS

Dear Mr Donaldson

Inadequate records

On [date], I contacted your Records Department [or other relevant name] in order to check on a number of items. I wished specifically to check on stock levels, shrinkage and goods damaged levels [or other relevant matters].

I found I was unable to obtain all the data I required because your records are incomplete. They are typically [number] days behind hand.

From our point of view, this is a very unsatisfactory situation as we do need up-to-date information to plan our production for the following week.

I should be grateful if you would investigate this problem and let me know what you propose to do to improve matters.

Yours sincerely

Comment

There are so many excuses that can be advanced for records being out of date that it is difficult to get effective action to improve the state of affairs. As with many other tricky letters, the one thing you do have to avoid when exasperated by others' inefficiency is to become abusive.

You should have a valid reason available for needing the information and should ask for the distributor to take action and to let you know what this is.

6

Staff

6.1 FAILURE OF APPLICATION FOR JOB

Dear Ms Brice

Application for [brief details of post applied for]

Thank you very much for your application for this post.

I very much regret, however, that on this occasion you have not been successful.

There were [number] applications for the post and the standard of applicants was very high. Regrettably, only one candidate could be successful and you should not feel that your non-selection was due to any failings on your part.

I wish you every success in your future applications. We should certainly be pleased to consider your submission for any further vacancies which we may advertise.

Yours sincerely

Comment

Many people find this one of the most difficult letters to write. You have to try to sound positive whilst at the same time giving someone news they do not really want to hear.

Some people content themselves with writing only the first two paragraphs, but this makes the letter too terse and unfeeling. You need to follow the inevitable bad news with some little explanation of the simple fact that only one candidate can succeed for each job. It does no harm to remind applicants of this.

Finally, you need to end on a positive note. Yours is, after all, not the only vacancy that will be advertised this year. Nor is there any harm in indicating that you will be quite happy to consider their application for any other jobs you might advertise in the future. You will not place yourself under an obligation to appoint them if you do this.

6.2 FIRST DISCIPLINARY WARNING

Dear Mrs Cummins

First written warning

You have already received two verbal warnings from [name] on [dates] about your timekeeping in recent weeks.

As we have failed to obtain from you either a satisfactory explanation for lateness or an improvement in your behaviour, I am now warning you that continued lapses in punctuality cannot be tolerated.

I look forward to seeing an immediate improvement in your timekeeping and will be keeping this matter under continuous review.

Yours sincerely

Comment

Legally, a person is entitled to two verbal warnings and one written warning before being dismissed. Most organisations will, however, go further than this in their efforts to secure an improvement in attitude and performance.

If we assume that we are going to be generous enough to give a total of three written warnings, the first one should refer to the verbal warnings already given. You should make clear the precise nature of the behaviour being disciplined and then issue the warning.

Finally, you should make it clear that you expect matters to improve and will keep a close eye on the situation.

6.3 SECOND DISCIPLINARY WARNING

Dear Ms Hartley

<u>Second written warning</u>

Since I wrote to you on [date] about your poor timekeeping, there has been no improvement in your behaviour. You will appreciate that this situation cannot be allowed to continue unchecked.

Under the relevant legislation, you are entitled to two verbal warnings and a written warning before being dismissed for the offence of which you are guilty. It is the policy of this company, however, to explore every possible course of action before resorting to this step. I am therefore giving you a further 14 days in which to improve your timekeeping to the standards quite reasonably expected by the company.

I hope you will realise the seriousness of the situation and respond accordingly.

Yours sincerely

Comment

This letter should begin by referring to the first to show that it is part of a continuing process.

You should point out that the person is receiving generous treatment in such a way that your lenient approach should not be taken as a sign of weakness. Set a deadline for improvement which is a reasonable one.

Finally, place the onus firmly on the reader of the letter to respond positively to your generosity.

6.4 FINAL DISCIPLINARY WARNING

Dear Mr Jackson

Final written warning

You have now received two verbal warnings and two written warnings about your timekeeping and the situation has not improved.

I therefore now have no alternative but to tell you that, unless your timekeeping over the next seven days meets the standards required, I shall issue you with a dismissal notice.

You must realise that the company has gone far beyond what is required by law in your case and that no further leniency can be shown. This is the final warning you will receive.

Yours sincerely

Comment

If matters come to this point, you have reached the end of the road and have to be quite firm. There is no way the blow can be softened now. This person has to realise that this is the last chance and that there will be no further leniency. You have done everything you could reasonably be expected to do in the circumstances.

You should give a tighter deadline for improvement than last time and should state the action that will follow if no improvement happens.

You should be quite specific that this is the final warning.

6.5 BEREAVEMENT

Dear Mrs Lewis

It was with considerable sorrow that I heard of your recent bereavement [give brief details].

Words are always inadequate at times like these, but I felt I had to write to assure you that we understand the sense of loss you must feel. I am sure that I am speaking on behalf of everyone here when I say that we send you our most sincere condolences.

Please contact me personally if there is any way in which we can be of assistance to you at this time.

Yours sincerely

Comment

91

This is perhaps the most personal of business letters. A heading, say the deceased's name, would be far too formal. It is not at all an easy letter to write. Times of loss are notoriously difficult to find words for. You have to strike a balance between saying enough and not saying so much that you rekindle the grief of the person you are writing to.

6.6 TOO MUCH ABSENCE THROUGH ILLNESS

Dear Mr Meek

I have been looking through our staff records and I note that in the past year you have had [number] days off work through illness. Indeed, the last date on which you were at work was [date].

I should be grateful, therefore, if you would make an appointment with the company doctor, in accordance with your contract of employment, for an examination. If you are unable to come to the office for this examination, we can make arrangements for the doctor to visit you at home.

Please contact me personally, or have someone contact me, if you are unable for any reason to make the necessary arrangements.

Yours sincerely

Comment

We have to assume that we are dealing with a genuinely sick person here. We may, of course, be dealing with a malingerer, but if we assume this to be the case we shall ultimately cause more trouble for ourselves than we can handle. If the matter eventually comes to dismissal proceedings, it will not look too good if it is obvious that we have been prejudiced in our approach to the individual concerned.

Since we are dealing with a sick person, we have to recognise that it might not be easy for them to do the sorts of things that normal, healthy people can do. They may not be able to make the journey to the office. They may not even be able to use the telephone. It may eventually be necessary for someone to call, but it will probably be best to send a letter like this first. Calling cold might be interpreted as snooping.

6.7 CONFIDENTIAL REFERENCE

Dear Mrs Park

<u>Reference for [name]</u>

Thank you for your letter of [date], requesting a confidential reference for [name] who has applied to you for the post of [details of post].

[Name] has worked for this company as [title of post] since [date]. During this time he/she has been responsible for [brief details]. He/she has had experience of [brief details].

I have always found [name] to be honest, trustworthy and reliable. He/she has always shown considerable enthusiasm for his/her work and has not been afraid to accept responsibility and to show initiative. If [name] has a fault it is [brief details if any exists].

So far as I am able to tell from the information you supplied about the post, I have every confidence that [name] will be able to perform the duties of [title of post] to a high standard. I have no hesitation in warmly recommending him/her for serious consideration for appointment.

Yours sincerely

Comment

Confidential references have to be written with some care. It is very tempting to give an unjustifiably good reference to someone you want to be rid of and a poor reference for someone you wish to keep. There is also the possibility that the reference might not be treated with proper discretion and that someone might see it who should not.

The language should be fairly formal in tone and positive wherever possible. If negative points have to be made, they should be balanced by whatever positive points are available. If, however, there are no positive points to be made, then you cannot escape from your responsibility to tell the truth

Words need to be chosen with care. 'Could not meet the standards set' reads better than 'He was incompetent'.

6.8 QUALIFIED REFERENCE

Dear Ms Walters

Thank you for your letter of [date] requesting a reference for [name] who has applied to you for the post of [state title].

[Name] worked for this company as [title of post] from [date] to [date]. During that time, I found him/her to be a person of integrity and reliability. He/she was usually conscientious in his/her work and spared no time or effort that was called for to ensure that the company's business was conducted with propriety.

However, he/she had to be disciplined on one occasion for [nature of offence]. Other than that, I had no complaints about his/her work.

I am confident that [name] possesses the personal qualities and abilities necessary to enable him/her to discharge the duties and responsibilities involved in the post you have advertised. I have no hesitation, therefore, in providing this reference as to his/her character and suitability and I support his/her application.

Yours sincerely

Comment

Where you wish to give a qualified reference for someone, what you do not say is at least as important as what you do say. You have to choose your words carefully and ensure that any adverse comment you make can be supported by evidence.

It is increasingly common these days for people to have access to statements made about them, especially those kept on record. You have to bear in mind that, even though you are giving your opinions in confidence, what you say may at some future date become known to the person you are writing about.

You are quite entitled, though, to give purely factual information about the person's past conduct. If, despite any shortcomings, you can still support the applicant, it is useful to do this, but not to be too enthusiastic in your wording.

6.9 LETTER OF APPLICATION

Dear Mr Menzies

Application for [title of post]

I wish to apply for the post of [title] with [name of company] and enclose a copy of my CV in support of my application.

At present, I am employed as [title of post] by [name of company], a position I have held since [date]. My duties have included [brief details].

In previous employment I have had experience of [brief details]. I now feel able to submit myself for consideration for posts of even greater responsibility.

The post for which I am applying appears to offer me the kinds of opportunities I am currently seeking for personal development and for being able to make a significant contribution to the company's success.

I can be available at any time for interview and I look forward to hearing from you in due course.

Yours sincerely

[Example of a curriculum vitae (CV)]

GORDON R. WAINWRIGHT
Personal Details

Age: 56   Status: Married, with three children.

Occupation: Freelance Writer and Lecturer

Previous   1985–1987 Manager, Sunderland Open Learning
Posts: 1968–1985 Head of Dept of English and Liberal
              Studies, then Head of General and Com-
              munity Education, then Head of Com-
              munication and Industrial Liaison,
              Wearside College, Sunderland

	1965–1968	Lecturer in English and General Studies, Hebburn Technical College.
	1961–1965	Asst Lecturer in English and General Studies, Hull College of Technology
	1959–1961	Asst Teacher, Manvers School, Nottingham

Qualifications: BA (Hons) in English, with American Studies, Nottingham University, 1958
BEd (with Commendation), Sunderland Polytechnic, 1976
Member, British Institute of Management, since 1966
Fellow, Royal Society of Arts, since 1970

Publications: 1968 *Towards Efficiency in Reading*, Cambridge University Press
1972 *Rapid Reading*, Heinemann
1979 *People and Communication*, Macdonald & Evans
1984 *Report Writing*, Management Update
1984 *People and Communication Workbook*, Macdonald & Evans
1985 *Body Language*, Hodder & Stoughton
1987 *Meetings and Committee Procedure*, Hodder & Stoughton
1992 *S.T.E.P.S for Success*, Mercury

Business Interests: Associate Consultant, British Institute of Management, since 1974
Consultant, Guardian Business Services, since 1987
Chairman, P.R.E. (Industrial & Leisure Complex) Ltd, since 1987

Community Service: Chairman, North of England Development Council, 1981–1986 (Member, 1977–1986)
Chairman, Economic Development Committee, Tyne & Wear County Council, 1978–1986 (Member, 1975–1986)
Member, Northumbria Tourist Board, 1981–1986
Member, North East Regional Airport Committee (Newcastle International Airport), 1981–1986

Personal
Interests:
Subjects on which I have published books and articles, travel, conducting briefings in subjects covered by my books (plus time creation, present-ation skills and other topics), and freelance writing (Member of Society of Authors and of Writers' Guild of Great Britain, since 1969)

Comment

The CV should tell the reader in a single page, or little more, the key information about you, your qualifications, your experience and your interests. I have used my own here as an example of what I mean.

The letter should state clearly the post you are applying for and highlight the points of particular relevance about which there is more detail in the CV.

The tone and style need to be positive without being pushy. You have to demonstrate your enthusiasm and to make it clear that you are not just seeking to further your own goals. You wish to make a contribution.

6.10 DECLINING TO GIVE FORMER EMPLOYEE A REFERENCE

Dear Mr Price

Thank you for your letter of [date] requesting a reference.

You will recall that when you left this company you did not resign but were dismissed for [nature of offence].

Under the circumstances, therefore, I regret that I am unable to supply you with the kind of reference you require. I should, however, be happy to supply any prospective employer with a confidential reference if required.

Yours sincerely

Comment

The danger with this kind of letter is that you either go into too much detail or you do not give enough. If the person had any common sense they would not have asked for a reference in the first place. Nor would they be wise to use your name for a confidential reference when you have refused them an open reference.

Make the grounds for your refusal clear, but do this as briefly as possible. Decline quickly and politely. This is not a letter to dwell over.

6.11 ASKING STAFF MEMBER TO RELOCATE

Dear Ms Rowntree

As you know, we are proposing to move your department to our new offices at [place]. The advantages of this move for the company have already been explained at several meetings with staff and their union representatives [where relevant].

The move means that it will be necessary to ask certain members of staff, of whom you are one, if they are willing to relocate to the new offices. We are very anxious to retain as many of our present staff as possible.

I should be grateful, therefore, if you would let me know by [date] whether or not you are willing to relocate. You should understand, of course, that if your answer is negative there will be no alternative employment available for you at your present location.

Please contact me personally if you would like to discuss the matter further or if there is any further information you require.

Yours sincerely

Comment

This kind of letter should always be preceded by as much discussion as is reasonably possible. Relocation is such a sensitive issue that attempts to rush it on the basis of getting something unpleasant out of the way as quickly as possible are almost always mistaken. Haste causes more problems than it solves.

You are here more placing on record than informing. The reader will know everything you are telling him/her, but there has to be a written record somewhere to show that you have done it.

6.12 CHANGING WORKING CONDITIONS

Dear Mrs Southern

As you know from your attendance at meetings held with staff over recent weeks, this company is moving to 24-hour working in your department. This involves the introduction of a shift system so that staff are available round the clock.

It is necessary, therefore, to change your working hours as follows:

[Give brief details of changes]

It is intended that these changes should be implemented from [date]. I should be grateful if you would let me have in writing your agreement to these changes. You should understand that if, for any reason, you are unable to accept the new hours of working there will unfortunately be no alternative employment we can offer you at this time.

Yours sincerely

Comment

Once again, we have a sensitive subject here and the best approach will be to make sure it has been properly talked through before you come around to writing a letter. This is one of those letters where you should already know what the response will be before you send it.

6.13 FORMER EMPLOYEE IN BREACH OF CONTRACT

Dear Mr Thorne

Breach of contract

You will recall that when you terminated your employment with this company a condition of your agreement with us was that you would not use materials the copyright of which was owned by the company.

It has come to my attention that you are, in fact, using in your present post materials in which we hold the copyright.

I should be grateful, therefore, if you would let me have your assurance in writing that this practice will cease forthwith. Unless I receive such an assurance within 14 days of the date of this letter, I shall place the matter in the hands of our company solicitors.

Yours sincerely

101

Comment

This is a very formal kind of letter. Where contracts are breached you have to be very careful that you do not say anything which could be used against you in court, for this is often where matters like this end up.

Be specific as to the nature of the offence and set a reasonable deadline for compliance with the original contract. If you do not receive a satisfactory reply within this period then you will have little alternative but to put the whole matter in the hands of the experts.

6.14 FOLLOW-UP TO EMPLOYEE MADE REDUNDANT

Dear Mrs Andrews

Further to our discussion on [date] concerning our action of having to terminate your employment on grounds of redundancy, I should like to thank you formally for your service to the company over [number] years.

As I explained, we had no alternative but to take the action that we did. This does not, of course, make matters any easier for us or for you. I hope you will be successful in obtaining alternative employment and I shall be happy to supply any references you may require.

If there is at any time any information or assistance I can supply, please contact me.

Yours sincerely

Comment

This letter will always follow discussions. It seeks to confirm what you have already agreed with the recipient and to place on record that you have in fact done this. It concludes by offering a direct line if the reader needs anything.

6.15 LETTER ABOUT PROMOTION PROSPECTS

Dear Mr Clayton

I should like to ask whether you would consider promoting me to [position].

I have worked for the company for [number] years now as [position]. During this time, when people have been away on holiday or absent through illness, I have undertaken additional duties as [briefly describe additional responsibilities].

The position of [title of post] will shortly become vacant, owing to the retirement of [name], and I should very much like you to consider me for this post.

You have all my personal details on file but if there is any further information you require before deciding whether to interview me, I should be very pleased to supply it.

Yours sincerely

103

Comment

This is by no means an easy letter to write for the kind of person who usually has to write it. They are not usually the stars whose light shines no matter what the competition. These are the ones who work solidly and reliably, willingly accepting whatever additional tasks are directed their way. They are not the ones who immediately spring to mind when promotion is in the offing.

For this kind of letter, you should be positive without appearing to sound your own trumpet too loudly. Show willingness to take on work. Show experience of accepting responsibility, which usually comes with accepting extra work. Show keenness without showing a ruthless determination to success.

Finally, you should ask for the person you are writing to to consider interviewing you and offer to let them have whatever other information they need to decide whether to do this. One small point: you will notice that 'whether' appears here on its own and not in the more usual 'whether or not' form. This is because when you are looking for a positive response from your reader the last thing you want to be doing is expressing yourself negatively. There is no need to plant the seeds of a refusal. Using negatives in expression increases the chances of a refusal; using a positive tone increases the chances of an acceptance.

6.16 LETTER ASKING FOR A TRANSFER TO ANOTHER DEPARTMENT

Dear Mr Flowers

I should be most grateful if you would consider me for transfer from my present post as [title of post] in [name of department] to that of [new post] in [name of new department], which I understand is to fall vacant soon.

I have worked for this company for [number] years and have always tried to give of my best. My immediate superior, [name], has praised me several times for my efforts. I have taken on additional work and responsibilities when people have been absent on holiday or through ill health.

Though I am very happy in my present post, I should like the opportunity to extend my experience and increase my responsibilities. I feel the new post would enable me to do this and to continue improving the contribution I can make to the company's success.

If there is any further information you require in addition to that in my personnel file, I should be happy to supply it.

Yours sincerely

Comment

This is another kind of letter where it is easy to press too hard. You should make it clear which post you are applying for. You should give some indication of your suitability for the post. It is worth making the point that you are by no means unhappy where you are, but that a move at this time will be in both your interests and the company's.

A level-headed, positive approach, showing willingness and exhibiting reasonable ambition are required here.

6.17 LETTER ASKING FOR UNPAID LEAVE OF ABSENCE

Dear Mr Haley

I should like to request leave of absence without pay on [date], in order to [brief details of reason for request].

I would have preferred to have made these arrangements on my normal day off, but unfortunately this has not proved possible because [briefly give reason].

If before [date again], I am able to make arrangements which do not require me to be absent from work I shall, of course, do this.

I should be most grateful for your sympathetic consideration of this request.

Yours sincerely

105

Comment

You might think that this is a fairly easy letter to write, but some people give inadequate explanation for the request whilst others go into far too much detail on the reasons for it. Some even see it as an occasion for writing to impress rather than express. I had one member of staff, years ago, who, whenever he applied for leave of absence began, 'With the auspices of my head of department, I wish to apply for leave of absence . . .'. 'With the approval of   ' or 'Under the auspices of . . .' I might have understood.

6.18 COMPLAINING ABOUT FACILITIES AT WORK

Dear Mrs Holcroft

Canteen facilities

We should like to draw your attention to the inadequate canteen facilities provided and ask that you investigate the problem with a view to bringing about improvements.

We would particularly like to draw your attention to the following points [these are examples only]:

1 At present, the canteen is only open from 12–2 p.m. and there are many members of staff who would like it to be open in the morning before work and in the early evening after work, for those who are taking part in company sporting and other activities.

2 There is a considerable queue in the canteen between about 12.30 and 1 p.m. and we feel that there should be some conscious attempt to stagger lunch breaks across departments.

3 The quality of the food leaves a lot to be desired as by the end of the opening period hot dishes are often cold and there are no sandwiches left.

4 The size of the portions is a source of complaint for many members of staff, especially those who are members of the sporting teams and burn up more energy than sedentary workers.

5 Prices are significantly higher than those charged at canteens at other companies in the city and many members of staff feel that the level of subsidy should be raised.

Yours sincerely

Comment

This would be a very difficult letter for an individual to write because then he or she would be inviting the wrath of those on high for daring to speak out. It is far better if it comes from a group of people who cannot easily be identified as trouble makers.

It is also more likely to be effective if it comes from a number of people because any reasonable management would not want what is the single most common source of complaints in any organisation to fester away unattended.

The canteen is the example used here, but the structure could be used for any other source of group complaint.

6.19 AN APPLICANT TESTED FOR A JOB

Dear Mr Kellett

Thank you for taking the test for employment at our main office yesterday.

We should be able to give you our decision on your application in about two weeks and we want you to know that we will be giving your application our fullest consideration. If, for some reason, we are unable to offer you a position at this time, we will keep your application and aptitude test on file so that we can inform you if a vacancy arises in the future.

Yours sincerely

Comment

Letters for job applicants are often regarded as routine, but they can be tricky if you wish to keep your options open. If you are too dismissive, the applicant may feel there is no hope of getting a job and be discouraged. If you are too warm, they may think a job is almost guaranteed and then be very disappointed if they do not get one.

If we are to show a genuine concern for people's feelings and act like responsible employers, we should not treat letters like this too lightly.

6.20 REFUSING A REQUEST FOR A RISE IN SALARY

Dear Mrs Metcalfe

Although the company appreciates all that you have pointed out in your letter, we do not believe a pay rise is in order at this time. It is our custom to review all employee benefits and salary and wage rates in July.

Certainly, at that time we shall consider you for a salary increase, providing the production figures for your department are significantly increased.

Yours sincerely

Comment

This, too, is the kind of letter often regarded as routine. It serves to illustrate the fact that just about any letter becomes tricky if you want to pitch it in just the right tone and style.

It helps if you can give the reader some hope for a favourable outcome, possibly tying it, as here, to an improvement in performance.

6.21 ANNOUNCEMENT OF REDUNDANCIES

Dear Mrs Barden

It is with the very greatest regret that I have to tell you that, owing to the current decline in the market, it has become necessary for this company to examine the possibility of offering voluntary redundancy to some of its employees.

At this stage, we do not know how many employees we shall need to release nor which departments will be most affected. Discussions have yet to take place with department heads and staff representatives.

However, if any members of staff wish to volunteer for redundancy, I should like to talk to them as soon as possible. If you are interested in this proposal, please contact me personally.

I shall send you further information about the situation as soon as it becomes available.

Yours sincerely

Comment

If this kind of letter has to be written at all, it is best written as soon as the need is known. It used to be the view that all talk of redundancy should be avoided and swift action taken at the last possible minute. This was because as soon as creditors got wind of trouble they would pull the plug and stop all credit. Now, however, so many businesses have had difficulties and so many have gone out of business that creditors tend to try to keep the ones that remain afloat as long as possible.

A great deal of discussion should follow, with the maximum amount of information available to everybody involved. If compulsory redundancies become necessary, people should know about the possibility as soon as is feasible.

The offer of personal discussions is necessary. No one should have to enter this kind of situation without knowing all the facts affecting their own personal fate.

6.22 MATERNITY LEAVE

Dear Mrs Graham

Thank you for your letter of [date], informing me that you will be applying for leave of absence in order to have your first child.

I should first of all like to congratulate you on behalf of the company and hope that you will have a trouble-free pregnancy.

As you have worked for the company for more than two years, you will be entitled to maternity pay at the standard rate for 18 weeks from [date]. If, however, you continue to work until the eleventh week before the baby is due and give us at least three weeks' written notice of absence, you will receive maternity pay at nine-tenths of your normal pay for the first six weeks of absence. After this, you will receive up to 12 weeks at the standard rate.

After the baby is born, you will have the right to return to your job if you inform us in writing of your wish to return within 29 weeks.

If you require further information or wish to discuss any matter concerning your maternity leave, please contact me personally.

Yours sincerely

Comment

For some reason many managers, mainly men, are a little embarrassed by subjects like this and find it difficult to find the right words to deal with the situation. If you stick to the facts and use straightforward language, avoiding rather coy references to 'the happy event' and such like, you will encounter few problems.

All you really need to do is state the main facts as simply and clearly as possible and then offer to talk over any other matters of concern. This discussion can always be handed over to another woman if a man feels that this would be more appropriate. These days, however, there is not the same taboo on discussing topics like this that there once was and it may be only the older manager who really needs some help to deal with the problem.

7

Inland Revenue and Customs & Excise

7.1 INLAND REVENUE FOR MORE TIME TO PAY

Dear Sirs

[Inland Revenue Reference Number]

I have received your assessment for our tax liability for the year [state which], the first instalment of which is due on [date].

Unfortunately, owing to unusual and particularly difficult trading conditions at the present time, I am unable to remit the full amount straight away. Cash flow projections improve for future months, but this quarter's figures are significantly down on the period for which the current tax payment is due.

Would it be at all possible for us to pay the amount owing on this occasion in five equal monthly instalments of [amount] and one of [amount]?

If this could be done, it would enable us to continue trading at our present level and take advantage of any upturn in the market which may occur. Of course, should conditions improve before we anticipate they will, this would enable us to pay the amount owing sooner.

I hope you will be able to look upon this request favourably and I look forward to hearing from you.

Yours faithfully

Comment

Nobody looks forward to dealing with the Inland Revenue. Since time immemorial tax men and women have been held in a mixture of fear, awe and hatred. Yet they are often not as difficult to deal with as many people imagine. If a business is going through a bad patch, it is not unknown for the Inland Revenue to allow tax to be paid in instalments rather than by the more conventional six-monthly method. The sting is, you pay interest on any tax owing after the due date.

The tone of a letter like this needs to be fairly formal and you have to plead your case. But there is no need to grovel. Simple language and straightforward facts will get the point across. Honesty about the reasons for the request is best. There is no need to go to great lengths inventing a story, which probably would not be believed anyway.

7.2 CUSTOMS & EXCISE ABOUT VAT PROBLEM

Dear Sirs

Liability for VAT on hotel expenses

I have been informed by one of my clients that I am charging them VAT incorrectly on hotel bills.

The practice I have adopted, and it is accepted by all my other clients, is to charge VAT on the amount which I actually pay to the hotel, even though this already includes a charge for VAT. My new client maintains that I should only charge them for the amount paid less VAT and then charge my VAT on this.

The problem I have with their approach is that it seems to me that I shall be out of pocket as I have already paid the full amount including VAT. If I only claim from them the amount less VAT and then add on VAT, this latter amount goes to you. This means that I shall have paid the full amount, but will only receive from them the full amount less VAT. I shall be out of pocket to the extent of the amount of VAT.

113

I should be most grateful if you would give me a written ruling on this matter which I may then send to their accounts department.

Yours faithfully

Comment

One problem in dealing with tax and duty authorities is that you can become involved in quite complicated matters. This seems to be the case here and yet it is quite a simple problem on which guidance is being sought.

The question is: in reclaiming expenses from clients, do you charge VAT on the whole amount you have laid out or on the amount less VAT?

The answer that will be received is that you charge VAT on the whole amount you have laid out, even though this already includes an amount of VAT.

As you can see, because of the technical nature of the point being dealt with, it is more than usually necessary to keep the language as simple as possible. Sentences should be short and the terminology should avoid jargon.

7.3 INLAND REVENUE ABOUT CLOTHING EXPENSES

Dear Sirs

[Inland Revenue Reference Number]

I should like to request a ruling on a claim for expenses which I wish to make.

My work involves making presentations to clients and attending meetings where personal appearance is an important factor in the success or failure of the enterprise. It is necessary, therefore, for me to wear a suit and all that accompanies this.

As I do not normally, during leisure time or at any other time when working, wear a suit, it seems to me that this should be regarded as a legitimate business expense. I note that you do make allowances for clothing costs for certain occupations already.

I would propose an allowance for the cost of purchasing one suit, one pair of shoes and a reasonable amount for socks, ties and underwear per year and for this to be recorded in my accounts as a business expense.

I look forward to hearing from you and I hope that you will give my request serious consideration as the amount involved, though not large, is significant.

Yours faithfully

Comment

It is often surprising what can be claimed as a business expense for tax purposes, though it does vary from one tax inspector to another. I have a friend who claims his TV rental and licence fee as business expenses. But then he does write television plays for a living.

Here you need a logical progression through the subject. First, you state the problem. Then you lay the basis for the claim. Then you make the claim and, finally, you ask for a response.

The potential for success lies in politeness, logic, evidence and keeping things simple. You have to make the reader believe that you are sincere and that you are being reasonable.

7.4 INLAND REVENUE ABOUT DELAY IN MAKING ASSESSMENT

Dear Sirs

Reference no. [state reference number]

I wrote to you on [date], concerning the delay in sending me an assessment of tax due for the year ending 5 April 19—.

So far, I have not received a reply and I am anxious that, since I am not responsible for the delay, I should not be incurring interest payments on tax paid late.

I should be grateful, therefore, if you would confirm that I shall not be charged interest on the overdue tax.

It would also be helpful if you could indicate how long it might be before I can expect to receive the assessment. If I have to make any appeal against the amount requested, this could further delay settlement.

Yours faithfully

115

Comment

This can be a difficult letter to write, if only because you are duty bound to do what you can to pay your tax on time, but this conflicts with a natural desire to keep your money in your own pocket for as long as possible. It will not earn any interest for you if it is in the Inland Revenue's account.

You must always be civil to the authorities, especially when they have such power to make your life unpleasant, but you need to do a certain amount of urging them to make a decision. This would be particularly important if they did decide you were liable for interest on the tax paid late.

7.5 HM CUSTOMS & EXCISE ABOUT THE TIMING OF A VAT INSPECTOR'S VISIT

Dear Sirs

Inspector's visit

Thank you for your letter of [date], proposing to visit these premises on [date] to inspect my VAT records.

Unfortunately, I shall be away on business in [name of town or city] for the whole of that week and would therefore ask if we could arrange an alternative mutually convenient date.

I shall be in this office on [give a selection of three or four dates]. It would be most helpful if you could select one of these and let me know which one you have chosen. It would also be helpful if you could indicate the approximate time I might expect the inspector so that I can have everything ready for him/her.

Yours faithfully

Comment

This can be a particular problem for the sole trader or for the person who runs a small business which takes him/her away from the office either for long periods or unexpectedly. Usually, VAT inspectors are quite human and understand such problems. A lot depends on how you treat them. Some people seem to think they can be rude to the faceless people of officialdom and get away with it. They can be as sensitive as the rest of us. If you cut them, do they not bleed?

8

Professional services

8.1 ACCOUNTANTS ABOUT DISPUTED FIGURES

Dear Mr Bridge

<u>Accounts for the year [state year]</u>

Thank you for completing these accounts for us once again. Your help is very much appreciated.

On checking through them, I have noted one or two amounts which seem to be at variance with the information we supplied. These are as follows:

[Briefly list items concerned, their amounts and your original amounts]

Nowhere does there appear to be any explanation for these variations. I should be grateful if you would let me have a detailed explanation for the changes with reasons. This would help us to understand the situation much more clearly.

Best wishes,

Yours sincerely

Comment

Many people are intimidated when dealing with professional people, especially if they are not professionals themselves. There really is no need to be overawed and to feel that such people cannot make mistakes. They can and they do. If you feel that they have made errors, tell them. As always, be polite and businesslike.

A numbered list of errors will help both you and them to check later that they have dealt with all your queries.

It is a good idea to start the letter with a pat on the back. This helps to prevent a negative reaction on their part to the possibility at this stage that you might be criticising them. If they do not satisfactorily explain the errors, you might criticise them, but not at this stage.

Finish on the note that you are seeking help and genuinely want to understand where you yourself might indeed have gone wrong.

8.2 SOLICITORS ABOUT SLOW RESPONSE

Dear Mr Dixon

[Brief description of matter in hand]

I am rather concerned that we have not heard from you about this since [date]. This does seem to be a long time for a response to be received.

As time passes, it is becoming increasingly urgent that we should make progress in order that our business may progress satisfactorily. Further delay could result in adverse effects upon the business.

I should be most grateful, therefore, if you would ensure that we have a reply from you within the next 14 days. If this causes you a problem, please contact me personally so that we may discuss the matter.

Yours sincerely

Comment

Solicitors are notoriously slow in dealing with matters. It is not a profession which seems to have much in the way of a sense of urgency. This may stem from a feeling that it is better to take your time and get it right rather than to hurry and get it wrong. There should, however, be limits and if you feel they are taking too long you should tell them.

You begin by expressing concern. Then you indicate the reason or reasons why you need an early response. Finally, you set a deadline and suggest that they contact you personally if they cannot meet this reasonable deadline for whatever reason.

It is not unusual with letters of this kind to write to the company rather than to an individual, but it is usually more effective if you can arrange matters so that you deal with the same person for all or most of the time. You should try to avoid situations where you keep getting moved from one person to another each time you contact them. Writing to known individuals is always easier than writing to anonymous organisations and you can avoid many problems with tricky letters altogether by following this simple rule.

8.3 SOLICITORS ABOUT HIGH CHARGES

Dear Mrs Gould

[Brief description of matter being dealt with]

Thank you for your letter of [date] and for the enclosed account for services rendered.

There do, however, seem to be some points which cause us concern. I note in particular the following charges which seem to be high and for which no satisfactory explanation appears:

[Give brief details of items and charges]

We should find it most helpful if you would explain the basis for these high charges and why they are, in fact, so high. I look forward to hearing from you within the next 14 days. If this presents any problems, please contact me personally so that we may discuss the matter.

Yours sincerely

119

Comment

Solicitors are not the only people who seem to charge highly for their services. Garages are nearly as bad. When this happens, you should not feel intimidated by the experts, but should politely ask why. It can often result in a revision and reduction of the total bill, which will clearly be welcome.

Once again, a numbered list will both help you to check that you have not overlooked anything and to check their response point by point. The more points you have to make, the greater the need for a numbered list becomes.

You should set a reasonable deadline. Most people, no matter how busy they are, should be able to respond within 14 days.

E

8.4 ASKING SOLICITORS' COMPLAINTS BUREAU TO INTERVENE IN DISPUTE WITH SOLICITORS

Dear Sirs

Dispute between [your name] and [solicitors' name]

On [date] we appointed [name of solicitors] to act on our behalf in the matter of [state nature of business solicitors have undertaken]. Over the last few weeks/months [select as appropriate] we have become increasingly concerned that the work is not being carried out to our satisfaction nor to what we would regard as normal professional standards of competence.

Specifically, our complaints about [name of solicitors] are:

[State complaints briefly]

We have written to them several times on this matter without success. I enclose copies of our correspondence.

We should be grateful if you would investigate this matter and let us know if you consider we have reasonable grounds for complaint and, if so, what you are able to do to assist us in securing a satisfactory outcome.

Yours faithfully

Comment

When a relationship with a solicitor, or any other professional, goes badly wrong you have to grit your teeth and be prepared to do something about it. In the case of solicitors, you may have to write to the Solicitors' Complaints Bureau.

The letter will probably be one of the most formal you will ever have to write, but the task can be easier if you follow a few simple rules.

Begin by making it clear just who and what you are complaining about. Follow this with a concise statement of the details of your complaint. Concise means, of course, not leaving anything of significance out, but also not putting in things which do not add materially to the substance. Enclose copies of any correspondence that is relevant. Close with your request that they should investigate this matter and ask for an assessment of your case and how they can help with it.

8.5 TO BANK MANAGER SEEKING LARGER OVERDRAFT

Dear Mr Hurst

At the present time, we have an overdraft facility for [amount] which has proved adequate for our needs in the past. Now, however, because of difficult but, we believe, temporary business conditions, this is proving insufficient for our needs.

We would, therefore, like to request an increase in our overdraft facility to [amount] for a period of six months, after which we should like to review it.

I enclose copies of our cash flow projections for the next 12 months from which you can see the urgent need for us to secure additional financing until conditions are expected to improve later in the period.

I should be most grateful for your sympathetic consideration of our request. If there is any further information you require or if you wish us to attend for interview at the bank, please contact me personally.

Yours sincerely

Comment

The closer and more personal your relationship with your bank manager, or anyone else from whom you are seeking help, the easier this letter is to write. It will, however, always be a little tricky because banks, like many other organisations, always seem to be more ready to help if they feel that you do not really need it.

It is important not to beg or grovel. State the problem and its temporary nature. If it is a longer term problem, it may be better not to stress this too much. Who can accurately predict the longer term anyway? Supply as much information as you can, especially if it helps to present your case in a positive light. Show willingness to talk things over. Most bank managers seem to love to talk. Do not, whatever the urgency for a decision, set a deadline.

8.6 BANK ABOUT DIRECT DEBITING ERRORS

Dear Mr Liddell

Direct debiting errors

On checking our latest bank statement, we have found a number of errors in the amounts deducted by means of certain direct debiting arrangements which we have undertaken.

Specifically, the errors are:

[Brief details, dates and amounts of errors]

We should be very grateful if you would investigate this matter and arrange to have any discrepancies rectified as soon as possible. If there are any procedures you can propose which should prevent such errors occurring in the future, we should be interested to hear of them.

Yours sincerely

Comment

It is very easy with this kind of letter to adopt an angry tone. You should avoid this. It is true that mistakes of this kind should not occur, but they do. You are more likely to secure speedy action if you state the facts clearly and succinctly.

The details of the errors, even if there are only one or two, are probably best set out in list or tabular form. This helps the bank to check quickly and makes it more likely that your letter will be dealt with when it arrives rather than being set on one side to be puzzled over later in the day.

It might be useful to end by asking if there is any way in which this kind of thing can be prevented from recurring.

8.7 REJECTING INSURANCE COMPANY'S DENIAL OF LIABILITY

Dear Sirs

[Brief description of claim]

We wrote to you on [date] submitting our claim for [brief description]. You replied on [date] stating that you were not liable under the terms of the insurance policy which we hold with you.

We dispute this for the following reasons:

[State reasons]

We have consulted [name] who is a recognised authority in insurance matters and his/her advice is that our claim is covered by the following clause/s in the contract:

[State relevant clause/s]

123

We would, therefore, ask you to reconsider our claim in the light of this evidence and arrange for it to be met in full.

We look forward to hearing from you as soon as possible.

Yours faithfully

Comment

This has to be a formal letter expressed in a tone which is, as my old English teacher used to say, serious without being solemn. State the facts clearly and concisely. Give reasons for your dispute. If there are several reasons, it might be useful to present them as a numbered list.

On a matter such as this, it is useful to obtain a professional opinion and to give details of this in the letter.

Refer to relevant clauses in the policy and restate your claim for payment. Do not set a deadline for a reply, but indicate that you do not expect to have to wait too long. If they do not reply within what you regard as a reasonable period, then the next letter will have to set a deadline. This will probably be because you are now going to appeal to the Insurance Ombudsman Bureau. See the letter to the Solicitors' Complaints Bureau (page 120) for guidelines.

8.8 BUILDING SOCIETY ABOUT MORTGAGE REPAYMENT PROBLEMS

Dear Sirs

[Mortgage reference number and address]

In the current difficult business climate, which we believe will be only temporary, we are experiencing problems in meeting the mortgage repayment required by our agreement with you.

We should like to request a moratorium on repayments for six months, by which time we expect trading conditions to be improving. Alternatively, we would ask that you consider rephasing the mortgage repayments over a longer term.

I must stress that we see this problem as purely temporary and that we are convinced there will be an upturn in business within the foreseeable future. We do, however, need to address our cash flow problems in the short term.

I should be most grateful if you would give sympathetic consideration to our request and if there is any further information you require, please contact me personally.

Yours faithfully

Comment

Things are always tricky when you are writing to anyone for assistance. How much do you prostrate yourself before them? The safest answer would seem to be as little as necessary.

Make your proposal for action and, where possible, indicate an alternative.

Stress the temporary nature of your difficulties for this will be the case in most instances. If they are permanent, it is not likely that you will remain in business for too long in any case.

End with a request for sympathetic consideration and make the usual offer of further information and a personal contact.

Property

9.1 TO LANDLORD APPEALING AGAINST RENT REVIEW

Dear Mr Thomson

<u>Rent review on [address]</u>

We have received your letter of [date], notifying us that, as a result of the recent rent review, our monthly rent in future will be [amount].

This seems to us to be excessive, bearing in mind the state of repair of the property, the facilities available and the current state of the rental market for commercial properties. You will be aware, of course, that many businesses have ceased to trade recently. One factor in the high rate of business failures has undoubtedly been the level of rents that businesses have been asked to pay.

In the light of all the above factors and in the light of the adverse effect on our business at this time, we would ask you to further review the rent you wish to charge us with a view to setting it at a more reasonable level which we would have a better chance of being able to afford.

Yours sincerely

Comment

This is a fairly formal letter so it needs a heading. The tone should be restrained. Faced with large increases in matters like rents, it is very easy to over-react. This will almost always be counter-productive.

State the reasons for your objections to the increase and hint, but do not at this stage state, that you might have to consider moving to somewhere more reasonable. A move should be a last resort if you cannot persuade the landlord to reduce his or her demands. No business needs unnecessary upheaval.

Ask for a further review in the light of your evidence and arguments, but do not set a deadline for a reply. You do not want an early reply, especially if you can continue paying at the present level until the results of the review are known.

9.2 FROM LANDLORD REJECTING APPEAL AGAINST RENT REVIEW

Dear Mrs Simpkins

Rent review on [address]

Thank you for your letter of [date], appealing against the rent review on these premises.

I have examined the situation and discussed it with my advisers and have come to the conclusion that the rent proposed is fair, taking into account all the circumstances. I regret, therefore, that I am unable to reduce the rent. The new rate will apply from [date].

Whilst it is true that market conditions are not easy at the moment, they will surely improve in the foreseeable future. Also, it is [number] years since the rent was last reviewed and the current level is below that being charged on comparable premises in the area.

I hope you will be able to accept the new figure and I look forward to seeing you continue as one of our tenants.

Yours sincerely

Comment

It is never easy having to increase someone's rent, but if you have to, then you have to. You should at least assure them that their appeal has been fully and properly considered and that there are good reasons why you have had to turn it down.

If it is some time since you last reviewed the rent, it is worth pointing this out to the tenant as they may not have fully realised how long they have been paying the current figure.

Finally, you should express the hope that the new figure will now be accepted and that they will continue to remain your tenants.

9.3 TO LANDLORD ABOUT REPAIRS NOT CARRIED OUT SATISFACTORILY

Dear Ms Mawson

Repairs to [address]

We wrote to you on [date] giving details of repairs that were necessary to the structure of these premises. These works were eventually carried out and completed by [date].

Upon examining the state of the repairs, we have discovered the following deficiencies and departures from the requirements which we specified as being necessary:

[Brief details of defects]

We have brought the attention of the builder to the work that still needs to be done and to the work which still needs to be brought up to the required standard, but he is reluctant to undertake further work without written instructions from you.

We should be grateful if you would write to the builder confirming that he is to carry out all necessary works to ensure that this property is brought up to the required standard.

Yours sincerely

Comment

Again, this is a fairly formal letter and it is best to keep the tone neutral and factual.

If there are many problems, a numbered list will be helpful to both you and the reader.

Make it clear what kind of action you expect to result. There will normally be no need for a deadline, but there is no harm in setting a reasonable one if you wish.

9.4 FROM LANDLORD ABOUT REPAIRS TO PROPERTY

Dear Mr Irving

Repairs to [address]

Thank you for your letter of [date], concerning repairs to the property you rent from us.

As you know, I have visited the premises with the builder who is carrying out the repairs on our behalf. We have examined all the work done so far and have concluded that it is satisfactory. We have, however, identified some minor items where we feel further work should be done and these will be attended to within the next few weeks when the builder is able to schedule the work.

I hope matters are now to your satisfaction as well and I look forward to your continuing as one of our most valued tenants.

If there are any further matters on which you would like us to take action, please contact us.

Yours sincerely

Comment

Perceptions of what is reasonable in the way of repairs are bound to differ between landlord and tenant. The landlord naturally wants to avoid unnecessary expenditure on property and the tenant wants to enjoy as comfortable use of the premises as possible.

Though the landlord has the upper hand, there is little to be gained by being too obstructive. You should be at pains to show that you have acted as reasonably as possible and taken the tenant's complaints seriously.

If you can identify some small, inexpensive sweeteners which will slightly enhance the tenant's comfort, this may well be sufficient to defuse their feelings of being badly done by.

9.5 TO LANDLORD FOR IMPROVEMENTS TO PROPERTY

Dear Mrs Edmondson

Proposed improvements to [address]

We have carried out an examination of these premises in consultation with [name of company], who are well known and well respected local surveyors. We have jointly identified a number of improvements to the property which we feel should be carried out and which fall within the responsibility of the landlord.

The improvements which we feel you should carry out as a matter of urgency are as follows:

[List and briefly describe improvements required]

We feel that these improvements are necessary to maintain the property at a level of repair proper for a modern commercial organisation. We look forward to hearing from you as soon as possible. If there is any further information you require or if you wish to arrange a site meeting at which we could discuss the proposed improvements in more detail, please contact me personally.

Yours sincerely

Comment

Here, you are writing a pro-active letter rather than a reactive letter. You want something to happen. In this case, it is worth reminding yourself that the best way of being persuasive is to write simply, positively, in the active voice and concisely.

If the improvements are not many nor complex, you could well include them in the text of the letter. If there are many, however, and they are quite complex, you should attach them to the letter on a separate sheet or sheets.

Give your reasons for wanting the improvements and close by suggesting a site meeting. It is almost always easier to resolve matters like this by a face to face discussion. A letter alone will not usually do the trick.

129

9.6 FROM LANDLORD REJECTING REQUEST FOR IMPROVEMENTS TO PROPERTY

Dear Mr Chambers

Proposed improvements to [address]

Thank you for your letter of [date], concerning proposed improvements to these premises.

As you know, I have visited the [shop/offices/factory] with our [architects/surveyors/builders] and examined the situation very carefully. As a result, I have concluded that there is no pressing need at this time to carry out the improvements you proposed. The condition of the premises satisfies all the current requirements for buildings of this type.

I regret, therefore, that I must decline your request for the improvements to be carried out. I will, however, keep the matter under review and will contact you again should the situation change.

Yours sincerely

Comment

The tricky aspect of this letter is that it can be useful to maintain a cordial relationship with tenants. For this reason, you need to let them down lightly. You should show that you have taken their request seriously and given some time to it.

In refusing their request, it can help to sweeten the pill if you leave the door open to reconsidering it at some point in the future. It does not help relationships to kill off all hope.

9.7 TO LANDLORD REQUESTING CHANGE OF USE OF PROPERTY

Dear Mr Bailey

Proposed change of use of [address]

As you know we have rented these premises since [date] and have been conducting business in them as [state nature of business].

Now, however, as a result of changes in the nature of the market and because we wish to pursue activities which contain a higher degree of profitability, we ask you to consider allowing us to change the use of the premises to [state nature of proposed new business].

We have contacted the relevant departments of the local authority and have been assured that this proposed change of use would not require the submission of further planning permission as the use would still be for commercial purposes. All that is required is your agreement as landlord to the change of use, as this is significantly different from the use for which we originally rented the premises.

If you would like further information about the nature of the new business or would like to discuss the matter further with us, please contact me personally.

Yours sincerely

Comment

Begin by stating the current situation and follow this by briefly outlining what it is that you wish to do. You need to be precise about exactly what the nature of the change of use is.

Briefly describe any other enquiries you have made or actions you have taken to support your proposed changes and indicate clearly what it is you want from the landlord. End with the usual offer of further information or a discussion.

131

9.8 FROM LANDLORD REFUSING CHANGE OF USE OF PROPERTY

Dear Ms Bell

Proposed change of use of property at [address]

Thank you for your letter of [date], concerning the proposed change of use of these premises.

When you entered into the agreement to occupy the [shop/offices/factory], it was made very clear that the premises were only to be used for [briefly state permitted use]. It was also made clear that we could not consider any material changes to this. The change you have proposed does, in fact, amount to a significant variation from the agreement because [briefly state reason].

I regret, therefore, that we cannot accede to your request. If you are unable to continue using the premises for the agreed purpose, it will be necessary for you to seek alternative accommodation.

We have several properties on our lists which would be suitable for the purposes you have in mind and if you would like to inspect some of these or receive further information about them, please contact me.

Yours sincerely

Comment

The problem here lies in the interpretation of what is a significant change of use. Landlord and tenant are unlikely to share the same view on this. You should make it quite clear that you have a sound reason for your decision. You should also make it clear that, if the tenant cannot continue to use the premises for the agreed purpose, they will have to look for somewhere more suitable.

This then allows you to introduce a positive point by offering to help them with this process. If you do not have suitable premises of your own, you could still offer to use your own contacts in the business to help them to find somewhere. You are bound to know more about the property business than most tenants will have the time to find out.

9.9 TO LANDLORD ABOUT ARRANGEMENTS FOR VIEWING BY NEW TENANTS

Dear Mr Adams

Viewing arrangements for prospective tenants

As you know, we shall be vacating these premises on [date] and moving to new ones.

We realise that you will need to show prospective tenants the property and will need access to the premises at times which it is not easy to predict. We do, however, need to be able to continue with our normal business until the date on which we shall be moving. Recently, the number of prospective tenants who have wanted to inspect the property in detail has led to some disruption of our activities.

We should like to ask if it is possible for you to restrict these visits to certain days or times and to let us have advance notice of them. Even if this notice was no more than a day or so ahead it would give us some opportunity to be prepared and ensure that access to all parts of the premises was possible without, as happens at the moment, our staff having to move goods at the last moment to enable certain parts of the building to be seen.

133

Please let us know if you will have any problems in restricting viewing in this way.

Yours sincerely

Comment

The problem here is that you are leaving and the landlord will be less interested in your difficulties than in getting someone to replace you. This means that you must go into a little detail about your discomfort.

You should not adopt too much of a complaining tone, but simply make it clear that you still have rights and these are being trespassed upon by prospective tenants getting under your feet at inconvenient times.

9.10 FROM LANDLORD ABOUT VIEWING ARRANGEMENTS FOR PROSPECTIVE TENANTS

Dear Mr Clark

Viewing arrangements for prospective tenants

You will be vacating [address] on [date] and moving to your new premises. This means that we shall need to appoint new tenants in your place.

We have already received several enquiries about the property and should like to begin the process of bringing prospective tenants to the site to allow them and their surveyors to inspect the facilities. We shall try to give you as much notice as possible of these visits so that it will minimise any disruption to your work. Sometimes, however, it may be necessary for us to arrive with very little notice.

I hope you will understand that, whilst we shall do our utmost to limit any disruption, it is essential for us to find a new tenant as quickly as possible so that we do not lose income by having premises standing empty for any length of time.

Please contact me personally if the visits do prove to be too disruptive.

Yours sincerely

Comment

The problem you have here is that you are almost inevitably going to upset someone's pattern of activity. They will not be pleased. You have to explain to them the need for these visits to take place and that you will do everything you can to minimise the disruption.

Nevertheless, you have to make the point that, if the premises stay empty after the present tenants leave, this will cost you money. Being business people themselves, they should readily understand the need to get a new tenant in as quickly as possible.

9.11 TO LANDLORD ABOUT PAYMENT PROBLEMS

Dear Mrs East

As you know, we have occupied these premises as your tenants since [date] and we have always made our rent payments on time.

Currently, however, we are experiencing some difficulties in obtaining payment from customers as quickly as we did in the past. This has led to a temporary cash flow problem as we adjust to the new situation.

We should like to ask if it will be possible to have a moratorium on the payment of rent for the next six months. If the amount that will be owing by the end of that period could be spread over the following 12 months this should enable us to avoid entering into permanent arrears. This would be a situation which both you and ourselves would wish to avoid.

We should be grateful for an early consideration of the proposal and look forward to hearing from you.

Yours sincerely

135

Comment

This is a problem which is occurring with increasing frequency and which shows no signs of easing within the foreseeable future. It needs to be tackled with firm proposals. Most people who are owed money will be more likely to consider delays in payments if they can feel that the situation is temporary, has arisen through no fault of your own and is being seriously tackled.

You also need to impress upon them the urgency for a review of your problem without exhibiting signs of panic.

9.12 FROM LANDLORD AGREEING TO A RESCHEDULING OF RENT PAYMENTS

Dear Mr Elliott

Rescheduling of rent payments on [address]

Thank you for your letter of [date], requesting a temporary rescheduling of your rent payments.

We have considered the matter carefully and are prepared to agree to your request on the terms you outlined.

You should understand, however, that this can only be a temporary arrangement and we would be looking for you to return to the normal pattern of payments at the end of the period. There is no possibility of this becoming a permanent arrears problem.

If you are able to return to a normal payment pattern sooner than you anticipate, we hope that you will make every effort to do this. We shall keep this matter under continuous review.

Yours sincerely

Comment

This situation can become tricky if you give any hint that you might be prepared to let things drift for longer than the minimum time for adjustment to be made. There should be encouragement to the tenant to get things sorted out. The danger in giving people more time in which to pay is that they might get used to having things a little easier. They should be prepared to make sacrifices to ensure that their essential commitments are met.

They should be made aware that you will be keeping an eye on things in case the position deteriorates further. It is one thing to try to help people in difficult times; it is quite another to give any sign of encouragement for slackness on their part.

Advertising and new business

10.1 A SPECIAL PROMOTION

Dear Mr Baker

[Title of special product or service]

If you could increase your efficiency and productivity and at the same time lower your costs, would you be interested?

It is because we think you would that we want you to know about [product or service].

At the present time, all businesses are looking for methods of reducing costs without harming profitability. [Product or service] helps you to do this.

[Briefly describe how product or service will benefit the customer]

In addition to all this, [product or service] possesses a unique additional benefit for your business. It is available for a limited period at a special discount price of [state price].

If this were not enough, we further guarantee that if, after trying [product or service] for seven days you are in any way dissatisfied with its performance, you can return it undamaged in its original packaging for a full, no questions asked refund.

Please return the enclosed post paid card today and you will receive [product or service] by return.

Yours sincerely

Comment

Most people, and businesses are no exception, receive so much junk mail these days that it can be very tricky getting a reader to progress beyond the first paragraph. For this reason, you should try to hook your reader right at the beginning. An effective way of achieving this is to pose a question to which you know the answer is bound to be 'Yes'.

You then need to tell your reader why you are bothering them and indicate the major benefits he or she will receive by attending to what you have to say. If you can, make a special offer, such as a discount.

Your readers need to be reassured that, if they do try out your product or service, they will not be exploited. A simple money back if not satisfied guarantee should do the trick.

You should not expect them to go to a lot of trouble to respond, so a post paid card for them to return will make life easier and a positive response consequently more likely.

10.2 SEEKING NEW CUSTOMERS (GENERAL APPEAL)

Dear Mr Craig

[Name of product range/service]

You may not know us, but we know enough about you to be pretty sure that you are the kind of person who will be interested in the products/services [select as appropriate] we have to offer.

I enclose a brochure which gives details of our services to you, the customer, as well as of our guarantee of satisfaction.

I would draw your attention in particular to [brief details of selected product or service].

Your business as [give brief details] could benefit from what we have to offer in many ways:

[List some of the ways in which customers benefit]

If you would like further information or would like a representative to call (none will unless you request it). Please contact me personally.

Yours sincerely

Comment

When you are looking for new business, it helps if you can convince your readers that you have gone to some trouble to find out about their business. You are not simply sending out the same blanket letter to everyone. These days, when nearly all businesses use word processors for letters, it is not difficult to tailor a letter specifically to each recipient, using a mail-merge facility.

A glossy enclosure may seem a bit of an extravagance, but it can help to establish a favourable image of you and your company in the reader's mind right from the start.

Finally, the letter should stress the benefits you are offering the reader and should tell them how they can obtain further information or talk to someone about their requirements.

10.3 SEEKING NEW CUSTOMERS (FOLLOW-UP)

Dear Mrs Gallagher

[Name of product/service]

Thank you very much for showing interest in [brief details of product/service].

I thought perhaps you might have placed an order with us by now. But then I thought that you might require further information. If so, please contact me personally.

Or perhaps you have found a similar product/service [specify as appropriate] at a more competitive price. We can match anyone else for price and even guarantee to beat any legitimately advertised price offered by other businesses for the same or equivalent product. Why not test us out if this is the reason?

Maybe you would like to buy, but not at this time. In this case, you may be interested in our deferred purchase scheme whereby the product/service [select] may be obtained now but does not have to be paid for until [date].

Whatever the reason, we don't want to lose you. Please contact me personally if there is any way in which I can be of assistance.

Yours sincerely

Comment

You have made contact with a new customer. They have shown interest and asked for further information. Then it has all gone quiet. No further response. How do you revive the contact?

You need to offer several 'hooks', based upon the likely reasons for the customer's inaction. They may want even more information, but simply have not got around to asking for it. A prompt may help.

They may have found it cheaper down the road. Many businesses in these highly competitive days will offer to beat any genuine price. You might try that.

Perhaps their cash flow will not permit purchase at the moment. You might consider offering a scheme similar to those often used by gas and electricity companies of supplying the goods now and accepting payment later.

Finally, offer a personal contact and make them feel they matter. Also, note that the contraction 'don't' is permissible in personal, informal letters like sales letters.

10.4 BIDDING FOR NEW BUSINESS

Dear Mr Jefferson

[Item/s being tendered for]

We wish to submit the enclosed quotation and tender for [state item/s being tendered for] in accordance with your normal terms and conditions, a copy of which we have received.

Our products/services [select] meet the specifications you requested and we believe that our price is highly competitive. We guarantee the satisfaction of all our customers both with the products/services [select] we supply and with our after-sales customer care.

If there is any further information that you require or if I can be of any assistance to you in reaching your decision, please contact me at any time.

Yours sincerely

Comment

This is a formal letter and should be businesslike and specific. Make it crystal clear what you are bidding for.

There is no need to be too pushy in this kind of letter because the decision will very often be made on the basis of price, assuming you have met all specifications. Be positive and offer further assistance, but there is no need to over-emphasise the point. This is not really a sales letter. If you have done your homework, you will have a pretty fair idea of whether your bid is likely to be accepted or not.

I have added the 'at any time' to this letter because very often, when people are considering major purchases, discussions may extend beyond normal business hours. It might just make the difference if they feel that if a query suddenly emerges they can telephone you regardless of the time. One hopes they would not do it at two in the morning, of course!

10.5 PLACING ADVERTISEMENT IN PUBLICATION ON SPECIAL TERMS

Dear Mr Washington

[Brief details of proposed advertisement]

We are considering placing the enclosed advertisement in a number of publications, of which yours is one.

We should be interested to know what terms you can offer us. We are especially interested in discounts for multiple insertions.

We are also interested in any special promotional rates which might currently be available, even if for different forms of advertisement from the one we have in mind.

I look forward to hearing from you.

Yours sincerely

142

Comment

The trick here is to whet the appetite sufficiently to make the other party prepared to consider something a little special. Most publications have special rates for special customers. You have to become one of those special customers.

Multiple insertions will attract the ad manager's attention. Steady business is always welcome.

They may, of course, already have a special supplement or feature in mind which might interest you. 'Different forms of advertisment' will make them think they might be able to sell you a full page. You have to make them think you are a 'live' prospect, even if your real intentions are quite modest.

10.6 PROPOSAL LETTER FOR A PROJECT

Dear Mrs Lunn

[Title of project]

I enclose a proposal for [title of project] which I should like to submit for your consideration.

The principal aim of the project is [brief details of purpose].

Benefits of the project are expected to include [list main benefits of the project].

Of particular interest, perhaps, are the following aspects of the project [give brief details].

If you require any further information, please contact me.

Yours sincerely

143

PROJECT PROPOSAL

Title:	[Title of project]
Target Market:	[Give brief details of the market that the project is aimed at].
Style and Approach:	[Describe how the project will be approached and how the work involved will be carried out].
Length:	[Give details of the duration of the project].
The Team Leader:	[Give details of the background, qualifications and experience of the team leader. You could also add details of any other key members of the team].
Analysis of Competition:	[For most projects, there will be competition from other organisations and this section should be devoted to an analysis of this competition and why your proposal is superior to theirs].
Unique Aspects of this Proposal:	[Identify as many points as you can on which your proposal offers a unique approach to whatever the problem is].
Completion by:	[State the completion date for the project].

Comment

This kind of letter can be quite brief as the meat is in the proposal itself. You do need, however, to give the reader a quick overview of the material they are about to read.

You need to tell them what the main aim of the project is, what the benefits are expected to be and what the special characteristics of the project are.

The proposal should then deal with things like (depending on the relevance to particular projects):

- what the project consists of
- why the project should be carried out
- how the project will be tackled
- who will carry the project out
- when it will be completed by

and it may also cover:

- where it will be carried out
- the unique aspects of this proposal
- an analysis of competing projects

10.7 A MORE FORMAL PROPOSAL LETTER

Here is an example of a more formal proposal for a specific project, given as an example pattern for you to use.

Dear Mr Barrett

Student support services

Thank you very much for your letter of 16 December 199–, concerning the availability of assistance to facilitate the development of student support services by identifying potential support services within local education authority areas.

I wish to confirm this authority's willingness to accept the proposal as described and I enclose the Summary Proposal for Development Project as requested.

The contractor's name will be Bridgetown Local Education Authority, the start date for the project will be 19 January 199–, the finish date will be 10 April 199–, the LEA covered by the project will be Bridgetown, the anticipated expenditure will be £[amount] and the name of the authority's senior executive responsible for the contract will be myself.

145

Please note that this matter is being dealt with, on my behalf, by Mr C. Galloway, Manager, Bridgetown Open Learning, 3 Brown Terrace, Bridgetown BR1 3PZ. Telephone: Bridgetown 799799.

Yours sincerely

PROPOSAL FOR DEVELOPMENT PROJECT: SUMMARY

CONTRACTOR: Bridgetown LEA

TITLE: Identification of Student Support Services

START DATE: 19 January 199–

COMPLETION DATE: 10 April 199–

AIMS AND OBJECTIVES: To identify possible agencies/centres able to provide services for students and to prepare recommendations in ways of organising support services within the Bridgetown LEA.

BACKGROUND: The new Bridgetown College will be providing courses from September 199–. The College is not a self-contained academic institution and will provide new learning opportunities by working with existing agencies in education. Courses require a carefully planned range of support services for students which the College will look primarily to existing local education and training agencies and centres to provide. The College will seek to work with local networks for the delivery of learning support services over defined areas. The first step is to identify potential providers of Support Services.

METHOD: Identification of existing and potential support for learning in the public, voluntary and private sectors throughout the Bridgetown LEA area. Discussions with relevant responsible organisations. Recommendations about the organisation of services to provide a comprehensive support service for College students. The College will be organising meetings to brief staff involved and to assess progress. An interim report will be made at the end of February.

OUTCOMES: A report to the College Development Unit before the end of the current financial year on the availability of support services in Bridgetown LEA; the reporting officer's recommendations for the delivery of support services for the College in that area; an action plan for the LEA to implement those recommendations affecting it and its institutions.

EXPENDITURE ELIGIBLE FOR REIMBURSEMENT: Appropriate salary costs together with superannuation and National Insurance, travel, subsistence and administrative costs, clerical/secretarial support up to a maximum of £[amount].

PAYMENT ARRANGEMENTS: A single payment will be made following a claim at the end of February in respect of actual expenditure in January and February and an estimated expenditure to the end of April.

10.8 A MORE DETAILED PROPOSAL

Here is an example of a more detailed proposal on a specific project, given as an example on which you can base your own.

Dear Mr Aston

Proposal for a report writing workshop

At the request of Mrs Davis of TCP Ltd, I enclose a proposal for a report writing workshop.

I hope I have included all the information you require, but if there is anything further you need please let me know.

With best wishes,

Yours sincerely

NORTH EAST TRAINING SERVICES
REPORT WRITING: PROPOSAL

29 August 199–

This document represents a proposal to run a one-day workshop in report writing for ABC Ltd. Workshop details may be subject to further refinement on the basis of subsequent discussions between the client and the workshop leader.

WORKSHOP OUTLINE

One-day Workshop

REPORT WRITING

Introduction: Reports play an increasingly important role in business today. In particular, major policy decisions are often made on the basis of recommendations contained in reports submitted to top management. By their very nature, most reports in business and industry flow upwards and thus a manager is often judged by the quality of the reports he or she produces.

Most managers have had no formal training in report writing and this workshop has been designed to fill that gap. Its purpose is to assist managers, and others concerned with writing reports for the use of management, to construct more effective reports and to ease for them the burden of report writing.

Objectives: The workshop will be concerned with:

1 The essential preparatory work necessary to define objectives and plan the overall approach.

2 The principles and techniques of effective writing in reports.

3 A step-by-step approach to the writing of reports which both saves time and increases effectiveness.

The workshop will also consider techniques in the collection of information, how to ensure good style and clarity of writing, and how to improve readability.

Methods: The workshop achieves its objectives by means of a simple combination of instruction, practice and discussion. Participants will receive a copy of *Report Writing* by Gordon R. Wainwright, published by Management Update (copy enclosed).

One day Workshop

REPORT WRITING
Programme

0930 Introduction
    Introductory exercise
    Reports: types and purposes

    Report Writing – 1: Preparation
    Terms of reference
    Reader analysis
    Objectives

    Collection of information
    Notemaking and the storage of information

Report writing – 2: Assessment
Incubation periods
Readiness to proceed
Report writing – 3: Planning
Type and form of report
Selection of information
Organisation of information
Organising the body of the report

1030 Coffee

1045 Report writing – 4: Expression
Rapid composition
Order of writing
Keeping to the plan
Principles and techniques of effective writing
Length of report
Illustrative material

Report writing – 5: Review   149
Checklist for report analysis
Assessing readability
Editing and presentation
Submission

1230 Lunch

1330 Practical session

Course members will work in groups on a case study

1515 Tea

1530 Review of the work done in the practical session

Concluding discussion

Close of workshop

WORKSHOP LEADER

Summary: Gordon R. Wainwright, BA, BEd, MBIM, FRSA,
            International Consultant in Human Resource
            Development, is the author of seven books on
            management communication skills. He has
            successfully led briefings and workshops with

managers from numerous industrial companies, major banks and finance houses, government departments, local authorities and many other multi-national and national organisations for over 25 years.

WORKSHOP NUMBERS

A maximum of 12 is envisaged.

FACILITIES AND EQUIPMENT

The provision of facilities and equipment is the responsibility of the client. Equipment required comprises:

- A room suitable to seat a group at tables arranged in a U-shape
- Overhead projector and screen
- Flipchart
- Two syndicate rooms unless main room is large enough for group work
- A plentiful supply of A4 lined writing paper and pens/pencils

150

DATE

17 November 199–

FEES

The workshop fee will be £[insert amount] per day + VAT.

The workshop leader's travel, overnight accommodation (on 16 November 199–) and incidental expenses will be charged at cost.

Copies of the book required for each participant in the workshop, *Report Writing* by Gordon R. Wainwright (Management Update Ltd, 2nd ed., 1990), will be supplied at £6.50 each.

11

The media and public relations

11.1 TO AN EDITOR TO INCREASE CHANCES OF PUBLICATION

Dear Mr Carter

Few people in this community realise just how much they depend on 151 [product or service]. It is particularly disappointing, therefore, to find that this receives so little attention from the media.

There is, for instance, negligible coverage on television and radio. Even the press rarely show any serious interest. Trade and professional publications are, it is true, more likely to contain information about [product or service]. Little of this, however, finds its way to the attention of the general public.

It is for these reasons that I should be grateful if you could spare an inch or two of your columns to allow me to bring the attention of your readers to this important subject.

Briefly, I should like to make the following points [briefly state your message].

Should any of your readers require further information, they may write to me at the above address. It would be very much appreciated if they would include a stamped addressed envelope.

Yours sincerely

F

Comment

Editors usually receive so many letters for publication that they cannot possibly print them all, even if they wanted to. You have to ensure that your letter at least gets read. You need to begin therefore with a point which will attract attention. Make it sound like the subject needs airing because of neglect or novelty. Editors are always looking for the unusual. Things that have been fully covered elsewhere will be of little interest unless they are sensational.

Make it clear that you can deal with your subject in a minimum of space. Many publications actually specify a 200 word limit for letters so that they can get more into the available space. Longer letters may well be cut without reference to the writer if they are printed.

When you make your points, make them briefly. If the subject warrants it, indicate where interested readers can get further information.

11.2 LETTER TO THE PRESS CORRECTING A MISLEADING REPORT

Dear Mr Ellison

<u>Subject of press report</u>

I was most disappointed to read your report in [column or feature title] on [date] about [brief details of subject of article].

I feel there are several inaccuracies in the article and should like to place on record the true facts. [Give details of errors with the true position after each one.]

Since the article you published presents this company in such an unfavourable light and since the matter is one of such considerable public concern, I hope you will seriously consider publishing a full retraction. At the very least, I should be grateful if you would publish this letter in your letters columns.

153

I look forward to hearing from you.

Yours sincerely

Comment

Here, we want to persuade somebody to do something they invariably prefer not to do. It is very difficult to get editors to print retractions or apologies unless there is a clear and present legal threat to them. If we do not wish or intend to resort to legal methods, then there is no point in being abusive. We have to show evidence that we have a reasonable grievance.

A numbered list may help here, especially if the correction to each error is paired with each error. You need to indicate that you feel you have a justified grievance, but there is no point in threatening any action which has no real hope of succeeding.

11.3 PRESS RELEASE LETTER

For immediate release

LOCAL COMPANY'S AMAZING NEW PRODUCT

[Name of company] have just announced an amazing new addition to their product range. They have been leaders in the field of battery manufacture for many years. Now their scientists have come up with something that will revolutionise the way we live.

They have invented a battery which is 10 times more powerful than any at present on the market. And it is one-quarter of the weight of conventional batteries.

The technology is such that the new battery can be made in almost any size and shape. It is also rechargeable simply by plugging it into the mains by means of a small attachment.

Prototypes have been tested in products as diverse as pocket computers and long distance lorries. In all cases they have performed beyond all expectations.

The new batteries are so light that even a heavy duty battery can be carried in the pocket. Batteries for computers will allow the new pocket machines to be operated for dozens of hours instead of the three or four hours possible at the moment.

For further details or to arrange photo opportunities, interviews and factory visits, please contact [name] on [telephone number].

Comment

Press releases should be written in such a way that they can, if required, be used almost unedited by the publications they are sent to. Journalists are busy people and will often welcome material which saves them a certain amount of work. There will always be other stories they can then turn their attention to.

Clearly, you must have a story worth telling, but you should not reveal the most important part of it straight away. Whet the reader's appetite in the opening paragraph.

Hit them with the news in the second paragraph. Explain why it is so special and why it is so beneficial in the third and subsequent paragraphs.

Finish by offering a contact for those who want to know more or see for themselves.

11.4 INVITATION TO OPENING OF NEW FACILITY

Dear Mrs Leech

[Brief details of new facility]

We would very sincerely like to invite you to send a reporter and camera operator to the opening of our new [title of facility]. A particularly novel and noteworthy feature of this facility is [brief details of main point of attraction or newsworthiness].

This will take place at [location] on [date] at [time].

The facility is to be opened by [name and title or position].

The opening ceremony will contain brief addresses by [names].

It will be followed by a buffet lunch/reception [specify].

Please let me know as soon as possible if you are able to send a representative as this will assist us greatly in determining the catering arrangements.

155

Yours sincerely

Comment

Many people mistakenly assume that it is the easiest thing in the world to get the media to attend a special event they have organised. The problem is that your special event is just one of several they will have been invited to. They cannot attend them all. You have to convince them that yours is the one that will attract the most interest from viewers, listeners and readers.

Highlight the unique nature or significance of the event. Stress anything that you feel is particularly newsworthy.

Make sure the details of location, date and time are accurate. It might even be worthwhile including a sketch map of how to get there. It is surprising how many reporters are ignorant of places outside their immediate area. They are rather like taxi drivers outside the London area. They may have a good knowledge of Newcastle, say, but will be quite lost in Sunderland, a mere 10 miles away.

If there are to be refreshments available, make this clear, especially if there is to be a free bar. Journalists in all media are notorious for liking their comforts.

11.5 DECLINING TV INTERVIEW REQUEST

Dear Ms Noble

Thank you very much for your invitation for us to participate in your programme, [title of programme].

Unfortunately, because of [major event or circumstances preventing acceptance] it is not possible for our managing director to be present on this occasion. Further, he/she feels that, owing to the importance of the issues which will be discussed, it would not be appropriate for him/her to nominate a substitute.

I am sorry I cannot be more helpful on this occasion, but perhaps there will be future opportunities on which we may be able to participate.

Yours sincerely

Comment

Just as it is difficult to attract the attention of the media, it is almost impossible to avoid it once attracted. Journalists will go to extraordinary lengths if they feel you are trying to hide something about a story which they consider it to be in the public interest to reveal.

If you have to turn down an interview request, you have to come up with a pretty substantial reason why. Simply saying that no one is available for comment will not do.

You should apologise, of course, and express the hope that you can be more helpful in future. None of this can be guaranteed to work, but it offers you your best chance of evading the glare of publicity.

11.6 LETTER TO RESIDENTS COMPLAINING OF PROBLEMS WITH A LOCAL FACTORY

Dear Mrs Ridley

Thank you very much for your letter of [date] about [subject of complaint].

I am very sorry that you feel that we have been negligent in our duty to the community of which we are a part. There was certainly no intention on our side to be anything other than good neighbours.

You complain about the following events which your members have recorded:

[Numbered list of complaints stated briefly]

I have consulted all the relevant departments and am assured by them that the position on each of your complaints is as follows:

[Numbered list of responses to complaints]

I hope this clarifies matters for your members, but if a representative delegation wishes to come to our offices to meet and discuss any outstanding problems, please let me know. If you prefer, it may be possible to arrange for a speaker to make a presentation on our activities and plans for the future at one of your meetings.

Yours sincerely

Comments

This is a firefighting letter. The writer of the original complaint is obviously up in arms about something. What for you may be a small irritation is for them the biggest problem they (and therefore, they will think, you) have. It has to be taken seriously or the problem will simply grow and fester, especially if the residents have already gone to the trouble of organising themselves to complain about your anti-social (as they see them) activities.

The best way to deal with any complaint is to avoid becoming too defensive or rejecting it out of hand. An apology early on in the letter, without admitting liability, is useful. It helps to restate the complaints in a numbered list. Your responses can then be similarly numbered for ease of reference. It helps to try to identify with the group on the basis that if they feel they have a problem, then you, as a responsible local company, also have a problem. A willingness to talk things over in some way should increase the chances, except with particularly entrenched opinions, of securing a mutually acceptable outcome.

11.7 DEALING WITH REQUESTS FOR GROUP VISITS

Dear Ms Sowerby

Thank you very much for your request for your group to visit our premises for a conducted tour.

Unfortunately, we are strictly limited in the number of such groups that we can accommodate within any given period of time. At present, we are fully booked until [date].

If you would like to arrange a visit after this date, please write to me again offering a selection of preferably three or four dates. Please note that the maximum group size is [number] persons and that the minimum age is [number] years.

Yours sincerely

158

Comment

Many people find it difficult to turn down requests for any kind of assistance, but sometimes you have to do it if you are to avoid being swamped by them. A common cause of this in any business which is operating a factory or process of interest is the group visit.

In response to a request, you have to make it clear that circumstances force you to limit the number of visits you can allow in any given period of time.

Get people to book well in advance and to give you a selection of dates on which they would like to visit. It is not a bad idea to place a limit on the size of each group and a minimum age. Not many businesses can survive for long the ravages of extremely enthusiastic, but extremely young, schoolchildren.

Seeking, extending and rejecting invitations

12.1 EXTENDING AN INVITATION TO SPEAK

Dear Mr Cunningham

I should very much like to extend to you an invitation to speak at one of our meetings/lunches [specify].

We meet on [day] at [venue] at [time]. Our speakers normally speak for [duration] and this is followed by questions and discussion. Normally, we expect about [number] of our members to attend.

If you are able to accept this invitation, I should be most grateful if you would let me know the subject of your talk and whether or not you will require any audio-visual equipment.

It would also be helpful if you could provide me with a few biographical details for the person who will be introducing you.

If there is any further information you require, please contact me.

Yours sincerely

Comment

A common problem with this kind of letter is the omission of a key detail, which the speaker may well overlook until the day of the event and then have problems. I give an example. Some time ago, I was invited to speak at a conference in Belfast. I was free so I agreed. My hosts sent me all the details and even supplied tickets for the flights. When I arrived at Aldergrove Airport I could find no reference in my documentation as to where I was staying that night. As it was a Sunday evening and my hosts had not supplied me with an emergency number, I was stranded. I had to make my own arrangements for overnight accommodation at a city centre hotel. I know I should have checked, but if my hosts had attended to detail I should not have needed to.

12.2 REJECTING AN INVITATION TO CONTRIBUTE TO CHARITY

Dear Mrs Hall

Thank you for your kind invitation for us to contribute to [name of charity].

Unfortunately, we receive so many requests of this nature that it simply is not possible to respond positively to all of them. We only have a small budget set aside for this purpose and at the present time this is fully committed.

It is therefore with regret that I have to decline your invitation on this occasion. I can only hope that you have more success with the other organisations you have approached. If the situation changes in the future, I shall certainly bear you in mind for a possible contribution.

Yours sincerely

Comment

It is not the easiest thing in the world to turn a charity down, but sometimes it is necessary. How can you let them down lightly? You have to point out that you already do as much as you can and that your resources are limited.

Always leave open the possibility of a future contribution because additional resources may become available or you may change your policy on which kinds of charities you support.

12.3 EXTENDING AN INVITATION TO ATTEND A FUNCTION

Dear Mr McAdam

We are holding a [title of function] on [date] at [time] at [location] and should very much like to extend to you and your partner [if relevant] an invitation to attend.

The [title of ceremony] will be performed by [person's name and title].

Among those who have also indicated their willingness to attend are [details of chief guests].

If you are able to accept this invitation, I should be grateful if you would sign and date the enclosed card and return it to me in the envelope provided by [date].

I look forward to meeting you on what I am sure will be a most successful occasion.

Yours sincerely

161

Comment

This letter should help to ensure that when you have to invite people to attend a function, you do not omit any necessary details.

It also helps to make sure that they let you know they are coming, if only to see that any catering arrangements will cope with the numbers expected. A post-paid reply card will serve the purpose and is worth the expense for your own peace of mind.

12.4 EXTENDING AN INVITATION TO SPONSOR

Dear Mr Morrison

We intend to hold a [title of sponsored event] on [date] at [location]. We expect proceedings to begin at [time].

Since the object of this exercise is to raise funds for [purpose], we are looking to local companies to sponsor some of the participants and should like to ask you to consider becoming one of these. Already the following have indicated their willingness to sponsor [list the main contributors].

Because of the local nature of this event, the evening newspaper and the local radio station have said that they will be attending and reporting on the event. This means that it should receive useful publicity for both participants and sponsors.

If you are willing to sponsor someone in this event, please complete the enclosed form and return it to me in the envelope provided by [date].

I sincerely hope you will be able to join with us in this enterprise.

Yours sincerely

Comment

In addition to giving precise details of event, date, location and time, you should make the purpose of the event clear before inviting the reader to participate. It is also useful to indicate who is already supporting the event as this may encourage others to join in.

If potential sponsors can be persuaded that they may obtain some free publicity, this might provide an additional incentive.

Make it easy for people to respond by again including a post-paid envelope for their reply. If you leave it open for people to reply in their own way, many of them simply will not reply at all.

12.5 REJECTING AN INVITATION TO PARTICIPATE IN AN EXHIBITION

Dear Ms Percival

Thank you for your invitation to us to take a stand at [name of exhibition].

Unfortunately, our budget allocation for this kind of activity is fully committed at present and we shall therefore not be able to accept.

I should, however, like to extend to you my best wishes for the success of the exhibition and hope you will still feel able to approach us for any future events that you organise.

Yours sincerely

Comment

163

It is as well with this kind of letter, especially as most exhibitions are organised by commercial organisations, not to give scope for a second approach which attempts to answer some of the reasons you have given for not participating. Be brief, but be polite.

Wish them well and do not close the door on possible involvement in future events.

12.6 SEEKING AN INVITATION TO SPEAK TO A GROUP

Dear Mrs Salisbury

We are a newly/well [specify as appropriate] established company in [name of district] and we like to promote close relations between ourselves and the local community.

I note from your programme of activities that you invite various organisations to speak to your members. We would like you to consider us when you are preparing your next programme.

We should be happy to provide a speaker, with appropriate audio-visual aids and handouts, on any evening convenient to your members. He/she would be pleased to speak on [offer a choice of relevant subjects].

If you are interested in this offer, please telephone me so that we can discuss the details of your requirements.

I look forward to hearing from you and enclose a stamped addressed envelope for your reply.

Yours sincerely

Comment

This can often be a delicate situation to deal with. People may suspect that all you want to do is to give them a sales pitch. It is important to make the choice of subjects an interesting one which does not push particular products. After all, people can ask questions about these if they wish when the talk is given. If they do not ask, there are always ways of working them in without being too blatant about it.

The tone needs to be fairly matter of fact and encouraging and a stamped addressed envelope will be useful for voluntary groups which are often very short of cash.

13

Internal letters and memos

13.1 MORALE BOOSTING

To: All members of staff   Date:
From: [Name and position]

Performance and efficiency

You will all appreciate that business conditions at the moment are far
from favourable to this company. Market conditions are particularly
difficult and competition for orders is fierce. It is essential that we all
do our utmost to see to it that the image of the company to those
outside it is the most favourable one possible.

One of the easiest ways of achieving this is to ensure that standards of
performance and efficiency in all departments are of the highest
possible order.

Production departments can help the company to maintain and
improve its position in the market by achieving targets for both
quantity and quality. This alone will make a major contribution to
ensuring that we maintain profitability and that jobs are safe.

Service departments can help by ensuring that they too are efficient,
especially those which deal directly with customers. They always
appreciate a friendly smile and a helpful attitude and this may make
all the difference between someone buying from us or going to one of
our competitors.

Staff at all levels in the company can make their contribution to
preserving and enhancing the success of what we do. Anyone who has

any ideas on further efforts or activities which would help the company to prosper will find that my door is always open – literally as well as metaphorically.

If anyone has an idea, but does not wish to approach me personally with it, I have asked all supervisory staff to make themselves similarly available whenever they can.

I hope everyone will respond positively to this appeal and to act as a little encouragement the company is prepared to pay up to [amount] for any idea which we successfully implement.

Comment

You should restrict internal communications of this kind, wherever possible, to one sheet of paper only. People will not read internal correspondence if it is lengthy or involved, unless it is quite clearly something on which they must take action. Here, they do not have to act, but we want them to. We should heed our general principles for being persuasive by keeping it simple, positive, active and concise.

One or two examples of the kinds of changes we are looking for will be helpful, as will the encouragement of involvement of those affected. If all ideas only come down from on high, people are less likely to take them up than if they have produced some of them themselves.

13.2 WARNING ON GENERAL POOR STANDARDS OF CUSTOMER SERVICE

To: All members of staff   Date:
         [or of a specified department]
From: [Name and position]

Standards of customer service

I have received a number of complaints from customers about our standards of customer service. Specifically, they have complained about:

[List main complaints]

Clearly, we have to improve upon this situation. Customers are the life blood of the company. Without them there would be no company. At a time when business conditions are so difficult, it is vital that we improve our customer service.

167

I would ask all staff to give this matter particular attention and to go out of their way to ensure that they satisfy all customers by the service they receive from us.

To encourage a more positive approach, I am creating an 'Employee of the Month' award which I will present to the employee who, in the opinion of a judging panel, exhibits the highest standard of customer care each month. There will be a modest cash prize and a small trophy for the individual to keep.

I hope that within a very short time I shall be able to congratulate every member of staff on their quality of customer service.

Comment

You have to be very careful when criticising people in any way to focus attention on their behaviour and not on them. Take the view that there is nothing wrong with the people, but they could improve what they do.

Be specific where you can about the kinds of behaviour that you wish to improve, but do not name offending individuals, as I saw done recently in a memo on a hotel staff notice board which I saw by accident after taking a wrong turning. The point is, you see, you can never be sure with semi-public documents like this that those who you would rather not see them will, in fact, see them.

13.3 ENCOURAGING INTER-DEPARTMENTAL COMPETITION

To: All members of staff   Date:
From: [Name and position]

Inter-departmental competition

We are all aware of the need to be as competitive as possible with other companies in our business. We do try to reward with incentives special efforts and successes in securing a greater market share than our competitors. But we need to do more.

I would like to introduce a scheme whereby departments compete with each other within the company. I think this will help to give us a generally sharper cutting edge when it comes to external competition. It will help to create a climate of competition within and without the company.

We shall need to operate different criteria for different departments. We cannot measure success in the same way in personnel as in sales or in production. It should not be impossible, however, to devise suitable standards appropriate to each department. I would suggest that the staff association/works council [specify as appropriate] should set up a sub-committee to establish and oversee a method of achieving this.

There will be a trophy for the winning department to display each month and I am open to suggestions for other ways in which we might reward success.

Please contact me personally if you have any ideas which you think we should consider.

Comment

A memo on its own is highly unlikely to motivate people to perform better, but if it is a part of a broader approach which uses other techniques like face to face one-on-one discussions, staff meetings of an open nature, some system of rewards for extra effort and the like, it might be useful.

Again, it helps to seek to involve people actively in the process and to recognise this when it happens.

13.4 GENERAL DISCIPLINARY WARNING

To: All members of staff   Date:
From: [Name and position]

Unauthorised use of photocopiers

Photocopiers and easy access to them are essential for the smooth running of our business. I have no wish to introduce a system of strict controls for their use. However, it is clear from the amount of materials we use that some staff copy far more than the company requires for efficient running.

At this stage, all I wish to do is to warn staff that the practice of copying anything for personal use must cease. If this fails, then I will have to consider restricting the use of copiers or even have them moved to a central location where they can be effectively supervised.

I regret having to contemplate doing this, but we must have more control over a potentially serious cost to the company. At the present time, we simply cannot afford to have lax procedures in this or in any other area of the company's activities.

169

Comment

General warnings are not easy to write if they have to achieve both an improvement in the situation and an avoidance of offending those who are not themselves guilty of the behaviour criticised.

In this common example, you state the problem briefly but clearly.

You make clear that, at this stage, this is no more than a warning to those who are guilty of the offence. You propose no action against them because those who are not guilty might feel this threatened them as well.

Express regret for having to take action and make it clear that it is genuine concern over cost implications which forces you to act and not an attitude of small-minded pettiness.

13.5 MAKING INSTRUCTIONS CLEAR

To: All members of staff   Date:
From: [Name and position]

Security alert

Unfortunately, these days it is necessary for all organisations to have clear procedures for dealing with security emergencies of various kinds. These are not quite the same as those we use in the event of fire. All staff will already be familiar with these as a result of our regular fire drills.

There is a special problem with security alerts and this relates to how we deal with visitors who might not be familiar with our normal procedures. It is necessary, therefore, for members of staff who have visitors if a security alert occurs to bear in mind certain points.

We must not do anything that will cause visitors to panic. The important thing is to clear the building as quickly and efficiently as possible without causing unnecessary alarm. Therefore, if you have a visitor at such a time, take him/her with you to your usual assembly point and inform your marshal of your visitor's name and who he/she represents. It is important that you remain calm yourself at all times and convey the clear impression to your visitor that you are in control of the situation.

In this way, not only can we ensure the safety of all staff, but of our visitors as well. At no time should visitors be left to fend for themselves. I am sure that I can count on the ready co-operation of all staff in this matter.

Comment

The delicate problem here is that you need to secure effective action without causing undue alarm. Events like security alerts are self-evidently stressful situations in which people tend either to panic or, if you have had a number of them, to react too slowly.

By focusing on the safety of the visitor, this places staff in a caring role which they are more likely to fulfil efficiently. It is always easier to operate with a clear head if you are responsible for someone else.

The last paragraph draws attention to the need to look for visitors who, for whatever reason, are on their own. This should overcome the problem of how staff who do not currently have visitors will behave. You achieve an improvement in staff alertness and speed of response without badgering them directly. It offers a novel approach to better security.

13.6 COMPLAINING ABOUT CONFUSED DEPARTMENTAL RESPONSIBILITIES

To: [Name and position]   Date:
From: [Name and position]

Responsibilities of [names] departments

Over recent weeks/months [specify] a number of difficulties have arisen because of the lack of clear demarcation between the responsibilities of [name] department and [name] department. These were [give brief details].

As a result, a number of customers have complained about the quality of service which we have provided for them. Clearly, we need to take urgent action to improve the situation.

I would suggest that we make the following changes to the respective responsibilities of [names] departments: [give brief details].

I would ask that the heads of department meet to discuss these proposals as soon as possible. At this meeting, it would be useful if they could bring with them any counter-proposals they may have.

171

Comment

Demarcation disputes and communications breakdowns are common in organisations of all kinds and they cannot be solved by an open letter or memo alone. You can, however, draw attention to the fact and suggest a way out. As this will never be universally acceptable, you need to suggest a meeting to try to resolve matters.

The fact that your solution will be challenged should not alarm you. Putting it forward will concentrate everyone else's minds. They will come up with their own solutions. By talking the problem through, you may find that you do not really need to make many changes at all. People will begin to make the present system work better. Communication breakdowns often arise out of not following agreed procedures. Demarcation disputes often come down to differing interpretations of roles and you can talk these through once they are out in the open.

13.7 REPLYING TO CANTEEN COMPLAINTS

To: [Name of individual or group making the complaint] Date:
From: [Name and position]

Catering arrangements

I have received several complaints about the canteen arrangements we provide for staff. These range over prices, size of helpings, quality of food, seating accommodation at rush times and the service given by the canteen staff.

As far as prices are concerned, we already subsidise these and the company cannot afford at present to subsidise them further. However, I have asked the canteen manager to review prices to see if we can cut any of them.

The size of helpings is difficult to deal with as my own enquiries reveal that not all members of staff find them inadequate. I have asked the manager to consider the possibility of a self-service procedure for certain basic items so that staff may take the differing quantities they need.

The quality of the food again is a rather subjective item as some members of staff are quite satisfied with it. I have asked the manager to explore alternative cooking methods to see if any improvements are possible through, say, grilling instead of frying.

Seating accommodation is necessarily limited, but I would ask all heads of department to see if we can achieve some lessening of pressure at certain times by staggering staff breaks.

The service given by the canteen staff is under constant review by the catering manager. He/she is to introduce brief staff training sessions, at times when the canteen is not in use, to encourage greater attention to presentation of food, methods of dealing with customers and generally presenting an efficient, friendly and helpful image.

I hope that these changes, where we can conveniently make them, will help to bring about improvements in the quality of our canteen service and, consequently, in staff satisfaction with it.

172

Comment

Few matters are more sensitive in most organisations than those involving canteen arrangements, so it is necessary to be particularly careful over the choice of language used.

Problems which may seem petty can grow and fester if not dealt with. They may also occupy so much time in office discussions that quality of work is affected. Bring them out into the open. Treat them seriously, without making them seem worse than they are. Suggest solutions where you can.

It is perhaps best not to encourage too much discussion of catering problems because, very often, what is a problem for one person another finds quite acceptable. You have to accept that you will never get it wholly right. Only call a meeting if the letter does not work and when you do, call it quickly. There is nothing to be gained by delay.

13.8 CHANGING CAR PARKING ARRANGEMENTS

To: All members of staff   Date:
From: [Name and position]

Visitors' car parking

As you know, facilities for car parking on-site are strictly limited and now, because of the increased number of visitors we receive, the situation has reached the point at which we must do something about it. It is vital to our business that we should deter no visitor from coming to see us because he or she feels that there will be nowhere to park. We must, therefore, create more spaces for visitor parking.

I have studied the present provision and have reached the conclusion that the only way we can achieve this is to reserve the area in front of the main office for visitor parking. This will create [number] new parking places for them. It will also have the advantage of being close to the main reception area.

As from [date], staff may not park in the places designated for visitors.

I realise that this will cause inconvenience, but we must ensure that at all times we are as easily accessible as possible to those who bring us our livelihood. I would ask for the full co-operation of staff in putting the new arrangements into effect.

174

Comment

After catering arrangements, there are few other matters which stir up stronger feelings in most organisations than car parking. It is another topic which requires the most sensitive handling and an appeal to people's better instincts.

Again, the approach needs to be positive and clear. What you propose will not be palatable, but it is necessary. Appeal for co-operation. After all, even the most recalcitrant employee should be able to see that potential customers have to have priority.

13.9 COMPANY PERFORMANCE

To: All members of staff   Date:
From: [Name and position]

Company performance this month/quarter/year [delete as necessary]

The period began well with several large orders from new customers. These enabled us to maintain production at the target levels for a while. Quality was maintained and customers expressed themselves well satisfied with our products and after-sales service. I congratulate staff on their important part in achieving this.

The later part of the period, however, did not go as well. Orders were down, there were production problems and after-sales service deteriorated, in the opinion of several major customers. Clearly, there is considerable room for improvement.

I am sure that the level of performance we achieved at the beginning of this period can be repeated, but it will call for an increased and sustained effort on the part of all staff. I shall be reviewing targets for the next period and will try to set them at realistic levels, bearing in mind the current state of the market.

Comment

The main problem with this kind of open letter/memo is with just how much information you give. Give too little and you will create resentment rather than greater efforts; give too much and it could be useful to competitors should it leak. It is perhaps best not to be too specific.

13.10 ANNOUNCING A REORGANISATION

To: All members of staff   Date:
From: [Name and position]

Proposed reorganisation

As you are all aware from the meetings we have had over the last few weeks, it has become necessary to make some changes to our organisational structure. This has arisen not only from the changing nature of the company as it has grown and developed, but also from the changes our main competitors have made to their organisational structures to fit them for the more difficult business environment in which we find ourselves.

After full consultations with all departments, I have decided that the new structure will come into effect on [date]. Most people seem to think that this will give them enough time to make the necessary preparations. If any unforeseen problems do arise, I should be grateful if they could be brought to my attention immediately.

I am sure that the new structure will make us more efficient and better able to compete in the market place. It will therefore increase our chances of being able to maintain our present labour force intact. If it works as well as our studies indicated it should, it may, in time, provide the essential basis we shall need for expansion.

I wish all staff the best of success within the new environment the new structure will create and look forward to being able to report at the end of this financial year that our decision to change was the right one.

Comment

Very few people like change. A letter/memo like this, therefore, needs to be thoroughly talked through beforehand. It should be careful in the language it uses and it should contain no surprises. It should really only be confirming what everybody already knows and accepts.

You should rarely announce change in writing, except in the kind of limited circumstances covered earlier in this chapter, but at some point it will need to be confirmed in writing for the record.

Business travel

14.1 SEEKING COMPENSATION FOR BOOKING ERRORS

Dear Sirs

Booking ref no. [state reference]

I wish to register a formal complaint about the travel arrangements we have recently made with your company and to claim compensation for the fact that we did not receive the kind of service for which we had paid the full price.

We booked with [travel agent]. We were to stay for [number] nights in [place] at the [name] hotel. The departure date was [date] and return was on [date].

On arrival at the hotel, we were informed that it was over-booked and that we would have to spend the first two nights of our trip in another hotel. The new hotel was the [name] Hotel which was not of the same standard.

Once at the [name of hotel], and to avoid further disruption, we requested to stay for the full period at that hotel. This proved impossible as that hotel also was over-booked later in the week. This meant that we had to return to the [name of first hotel] on [day]. All the disruption was making it very difficult to concentrate on business, which was after all the purpose of the trip.

We were offered taxis to effect the necessary transfers but, as we had hired a car, it would not have been convenient to accept. Thus, the to-ing and fro-ing involved us not only in disruption of our business trip but also in a certain amount of expense.

When we returned to the [name of first hotel] on [day], our rooms were not ready. We left our luggage at the hotel and returned later in the afternoon. The rooms were still not ready. At about 5 p.m., when the rooms were ready, our luggage had disappeared from the luggage room. It turned out eventually that the luggage had been loaded by mistake on to an Italian coach which was going to tour [place] before taking its party to the airport. We did not receive our cases until after 7 p.m., by which time we were well in need of a shower and a change of clothing.

I was also surprised and disappointed that, although both hotels belonged to [name of group], my Gold Card counted for nothing. Its only value was for paying the 'extras' bills.

In the circumstances, it seems to me reasonable that for the use of my car to move us from one hotel to another and back, the temporary inconvenience and worry of lost luggage and for the meals we had to purchase on the return journey, a compensation claim is justified. We had, after all, paid the full price and we did not receive the kind of service we had paid for in the hotel we specifically requested.

I look forward to hearing from you.

Yours faithfully

Comment

Travel arrangements can so easily go wrong that, often, when you write to complain you are likely to receive a standard reply in return. The trick here is in persistence and detail. You may have to be prepared to write more than once and in increasingly strong terms.

The more specific you can be about what went wrong, the better and I have therefore given some fairly typical examples in the letter above which you may find useful.

14.2 ERRORS IN HOTEL BILL

Dear Sirs

I stayed at [name] hotel on [dates] and when I left took advantage of the express check-out facility. I have now received my copy of the bill which you charged to my credit card and was astonished to find certain items on it which I had not incurred.

I refer specifically to charges for room service, newspapers and the mini-bar, none of which I used. You have also charged me for an additional night's accommodation on [date] by which time I was in fact back at home.

Please amend the bill accordingly and make the necessary credit against my card.

I look forward to hearing from you by return that this has been done.

Yours faithfully

Comment

It is becoming increasingly common for business people in a hurry to use the express check-out facilities that many hotel groups provide. The hazards are clear but the remedies less so. If you are not there in person to argue the point, it is easy to be fobbed off. For this reason, your tone has to be firm and assured, without being abusive. There is no point in any letter of complaint in being abusive. After all, in this kind of instance, they have you at a disadvantage in that they already have your money.

Keep calm and record all the details accurately, varying them as necessary from the details given here. Send copies of any relevant receipts that support your claim. Impress upon them the urgency of a reply and follow this up with a telephone call if they do not reply within a reasonable number of days.

14.3 NOT RECEIVING THE SERVICE PAID FOR

Dear Sirs

I recently travelled by first class rail from [place] to [place]. My principal reason for doing this was to have more space in which to work during the journey. I was surprised, therefore, to find that during the last 20 minutes of the journey passengers were coming from standard class into first class.

This happened, I believe, because first class accommodation was at the front of the train and those passengers wanted a quicker exit on arrival. It meant, however, that my work was almost totally disrupted at a time when I was trying to finish a task before the end of the journey.

I feel that, as there is a senior conductor on board, he/she should take action to ensure that this practice is prevented in future.

Yours faithfully

Comment

The tricky part here, of course, is that you will receive a bland public relations reply which says something like:

> Our objective is to run a customer-friendly company for all our passengers. We will ask the senior conductor to make an announcement to the effect that standard ticket holders must not encroach on first class accommodation. We are confident that such a positive request from the senior conductor will deter the vast majority, who were probably unaware that their action annoyed the occupants.

And that is an actual reply.

Your problem is to secure effective action. The letter above should help, but for situations like this it is often better to enlist the support and signatures of as substantial a number of other travellers as possible.

Index

■

181